Senior Year

---

a memoir

For information address:
J2B Publishing LLC
4251 Columbia Park Road
Pomfret, MD 20675
www.J2BLLC.com

Printed and bound in the United States of America.

This book is set in Garamond.

ISBN: 978-1-954682-02-3

Copyright

Senior Year

a memoir

Kelley Dietsch Smith

 J2B Publishing

For Steve,
Garrott, Brennen, and Julia—

you are my happily ever after.

with every thought
and with every breath

~Martin Gore, "Somebody"

Prologue

___

They say it's a fairy tale
how we began our life together
and I can see why
some people would think that.

There was
once upon a time
30 years or so ago
a carefree girl with great dreams
and a creative boy with immense potential
who fell prey
to a timeless temptation
making a fateful error
and creating a lot of
pain
loss
shame
and regret

that was overcome

by love —
a lot of love
from a lot of people.

I suppose the fairy tale feeling
comes mostly from
the happily ever after part.
And really it was.

And still is.

Maybe they're not completely wrong
when they say
the story of my senior year
is like a fairy tale.

JULY 1987

———

The summer of '87
is going to be the best summer
of my life.
I've done everything right
so far
and I've earned it.

My resume of adult-approved activities and accomplishments is long:

high grades in honors classes
(SMART)

a job for my own spending money
(RESPONSIBLE)

household chores
(HELPFUL)

a nice group of friends
(SOCIABLE)

a polite boyfriend
(LOYAL)

volunteer work
(GENEROUS)

my own car
(INDEPENDENT)

church on Sundays
(RESPECTFUL)

varsity sports
(ATHLETIC)

college bound
(AMBITIOUS)

Equals:

All Around Good Girl
(COMPLIANT)

So I am free.

To shop and have lunch with Jenny, Julie, and Becky.
Go to concerts with Steve.
Take trips to the city and the beach.
Movies.
Parties.
Bonfires.

I really believe it will be
The
Best
Summer
Ever.

We met when we were 14
at Shannon's Valentine slumber party
which got boring with just us four girls
so she called Brian.

"Sure," she said, "you can bring a friend."

Steve was quiet, but really funny
if you paid attention.

We played Truth or Dare
and Shannon dared him to wear my earring.
He wrapped the gold hook over the top of his ear
so the pastel triangle dangled over the hole.
I thought his ear was a perfect shape and size
hugging closely to his head with no bizarre bumps or curls.

Then Robin dared me to put a piece of ice from the sidewalk
in my underwear.
I saw him notice the peek of black lace
when I opened the top button of my pants.
I smiled at him.

It wasn't until junior year
after he drove me home from field hockey practice
that he asked me out on a date.
We ate pizza and played Putt-Putt
and then squeezed close together
for a series of silly poses in a photo booth.

One night, two weeks later
under the tree in his best friend's front yard
he kissed me.
I was thrilled by the scratch
of the skin above his lip
against mine.

Later, he only smiled
squinting his pale green eyes
and kissed me again

when I confessed that I already loved him.

Steve taught me
about music
pro sports
and comic book heroes.
He serenaded me with his poetry
and made me my first mixtape.

Now
his hand always seeks mine
and he laughs
when I shoot him my cat eyes.
He has tattooed "RED"
on the back of his left hand with a Sharpie
in homage to my gold and copper hair
and tells me I am beautiful.

He's smart.
He's loyal.
He's romantic.
He's creative.
He's funny.
He's generous.

He's mine.

And I am his.

Family vacations
are usually spent visiting our cousins.
All eight of us
driving to Pennsylvania or Nebraska
forced to touch thighs and elbows
for never-ending hours
or even days
fighting off encroachments
on my coveted window seat.

But this year
my parents rented a house at Rehoboth Beach
only a few hours away
for a whole week.

And we're allowed to bring a friend.

Steve and I drive there together
in my 69 Dodge Dart
that I bought with my own money.

My dad found it
in the newspaper for $750.
He said it was in great condition
and was big enough to protect me in an accident.
(The convertible Spider I wanted
was declared "the size of a roller skate"
which would ensure my early death.)

The Dart is long and white
with a hard, black top and Crayola-blue interior.
It doesn't have air conditioning
or FM radio.
There is no power steering
power windows
or power anything.
But it's completely mine.

My sister Mary and her friend Emily
are in the back seat.

The windows are rolled down all the way
and our hair whips around our heads
frantic to escape with the wind.

We all sing along to a mixtape
playing on Steve's boombox
between us on the front seat.
Steve's foot is up on the dash
and his arm is resting on the window frame.
He wears his Astros hat backwards
his smile as wide as the brim.

"This car is the perfect beach-mobile," he says.

The beach house
is filled to the roof with everyone—
my parents
my brothers and sisters
our friends
the dog
and even a couple of cousins from Delaware.

The rooms are stuffed with everything—
duffel bags and coolers
sleeping bags and flip-flops
towels and bottles of sunscreen
all dusted in a fine grit.

We spend all day on the beach
returning to the house sunburned and dehydrated
hair crunchy with sand and salt.

The hot water in the shower
stings my bright pink skin
which is splotched with large, sun-soaked freckles.

The door opens
sucking the steam out
as Steve slips into the tiny bathroom.
I can't
see his face
through the beveled shower door.

"What are you doing?" I whisper urgently.

"Everyone's still at the beach," he answers
turning the lock on the door.

My heart is pounding.
Fear and excitement
at the same time.

"How about we conserve water?" Steve says
as he pulls his t-shirt over his head

and begins to slide his swim trunks
down his thighs.

I laugh
as I push open the shower door
and pull him to me.

His air condition-cooled skin
raises goosebumps on mine.
His lips are sun-swollen and salty.
I run my hands over his back
from shoulder blades to the smooth up-curve of his hips.
Pausing there, I pull his to mine.
Our teeth bump
as our lips, open and pressed together
spread into smiles.
He runs his fingertips up the outside of my thigh
tracing a burning trail across my hip crease
and along my groin
and then deftly slips them between my legs.

In the afternoon
we take the canoe out on the canal.
Steve and I stab the water
with the heavy wooden paddles
while Mary and Emily chant

> *Left.*
> *Left.*
> *Left, right, left.*
> *I left my wife*
> *and 48 children*
> *alone in the kitchen*
> *in starving condition*
> *with nothing but gingerbread*
> *left.*
> *Left.*
> *Left, right, left.*

Steve slaps the paddle on the water
splashing the girls
until they squeal.
Sparkling droplets cling to
his sun-bleached hair
and the corners of his eyes crinkle
with a mischievous glee
that makes my heart squeeze
in my chest.

In the evening
we use string and bubblegum
to catch crabs in the canal
collecting them like seashells
in a bucket.

We toss them into a giant, shiny pot
covering their blue backs
with Old Bay seasoning.
Quickly clapping on the lid
we grimace
as the clicking claws
tap musically against the sides
then slow
and stop altogether.

At night
he sleeps in a bedroom
with two of my little brothers.
I slide out of my own bed
and sneak silently
to the foot of his.
He wakes
with the touch
of my hand on his ankle
and lifts the covers.
Wordlessly
we rock and sigh
and I return to bed
with the burning
temporarily quelled.

People often stare at my family
when we're all out together.

It's unusually large
with six kids, like the Brady Bunch
three boys and three girls.

Colleen
    Kelley
        Ryan
            Mary
                Michael
                    Andrew

And four of us
have some shade of red hair
which makes us stick out even more.

When I was younger, I always enjoyed the attention
people gave us
not realizing that maybe our family
appeared a little freakish to them.

"Are you Roman Catholic?"
is often the first question adults ask us.

I never understood how they could tell.
It's not like we were carrying rosaries.
Then I learned about the no-birth-control rule
and it all made sense.

Dinner at the Dietsch house
is a spectacle of barely controlled chaos.
It's officially scheduled to occur promptly every evening
as soon as my dad gets home from work.
But with all the comings and goings of six children
and my mom busy
working and volunteering
outside of the house more and more
meal preparation often feels like the frenzied scurrying
of a theater cast who has misplaced their lead actor
moments before the curtains are drawn back.

We pretend that our casual pacings
through the kitchen are a coincidence of timing
while covertly trying to discover
who is cooking
what is on the menu
when it will be ready
and who will be there to eat it.

If you make the mistake of wondering
any of these thoughts aloud
you will immediately find yourself
a member of the prep crew.

As Dad settles into his chair at the head of the table
the rest of us are already waiting
in our assigned places.
Along one side
the little kids squeeze elbow to elbow onto a long bench.
The older kids get their own chairs
on the opposite side.
Ryan, only the third eldest
is sandwiched between his big sisters.
The seat on the end is reserved for Mom.

The dinner plates are stacked high
directly in front of my father
with the steaming serving dishes all placed within his reach
like his own personal buffet.

Dad plates up each of our portions
and then passes it to the child on his left.
It continues clockwise around the table
until it reaches the child
directly to his right.

Everyone eats what is put in front of them.
Family members may petition Dad
for larger or smaller helpings
but there are no omissions or substitutions.
He doesn't even pause to ask for input from guests.

We must wait until everyone has their plate
and we have prayed
before anyone can eat.
At "Amen", there is an explosion of noise and commotion
forks and knives scraping plates and teeth
requests for condiments
and multiple simultaneous conversations.
Dietsch dinners are intense but quick events.
If you don't eat fast, you don't get seconds
so there is no leisurely enjoyment of the food's flavors.

That's not to say bad manners will be tolerated.
"Please" and "thank you" are required.
You will be reprimanded
for holding your fork like a shovel
or chewing with your mouth open.
There will be no hats at the table
no matter what state your hair is in
and you must ask permission to be excused
when you are finished.

The first time Steve joined my family for a meal
I think he was so stunned that he hardly ate anything.

I sat with him after everyone had finished
and gotten up to start the dishes
so that he could eat a little bit in relative peace and calm
after his heart stopped racing.

As my little brother Andrew cleared the table
Steve leaned over to me and whispered
"What the hell just happened?
I feel like I was thrown into Mad Max's Thunderdome!"

"You'll get used to it," I said.

And he did.
It wasn't long before
he was jousting with the rest of us
for the last dinner roll.

Jenny is my best friend

or she was
before I was with Steve.

Jenny was my first friend
when I moved to Maryland in ninth grade.
I was scared
and lonely
and lost
in the giant public junior high school.
I couldn't even go to the *real* high school with my older sister.

After six years of wearing a plaid uniform skirt
in a tiny southern Catholic school, with one class per grade
I was completely unprepared
to be a member of the largest class in the state.
I used to be popular, a big fish in a little pond.
Now I was plankton in the ocean.

It was culture shock.
I didn't know what to wear or how to fix my hair.
I didn't know what was cool and popular.
I embarrassed myself every time I opened my mouth.

Me: I have a compact just like that!

Her: So what? Everybody does.

Me: Oh.

I begged my parents to send me to Holy Cross
but it was too expensive and too far away.
I didn't know
how to be
in public school.

I'd never been without friends.
I was desperate.

I decided to try out for the girls' soccer team.

And that's how I met Jenny—
tying our cleats in the locker room before the first try-out.
I found out later
that she was also feeling a little lost
even though she'd lived in Gaithersburg her whole life.
All her best friends went to the other junior high in town
and her parents were recently divorced.
She needed a friend too.

"Where are you from? You kind of have an accent,"
she asked after I told her my name.

"Charleston, South Carolina.
My dad was stationed at the Air Force base
but I'm not really from there.
We aren't Southerners."

I was anxious to escape
from any Confederate connections.
My D.C. suburban classmates barely held in their scorn
whenever I carelessly let my adopted drawl slip into the conversation.

Me: So what did y'all put for the answer to number one?

Her (tittering behind her hand): Well, I don't know about the rest of "y'all"
(mocking smile), but I got negative three.

Her friend (giggling): Yeah, me too.

Me (keeping my eyes on my paper): Okay.

I quickly learned to drop the Low Country slang.

I connected the ends of the Velcro band behind my calf
securing the shin guard in place.
Jenny smoothed her hair back with both hands
and tied it with an elastic band.

"Have you played soccer before?" she asked me.

"Yeah, but not on an all-girls' team.
They didn't have those in Charleston.
Girls had to play on the boys' teams."

"That sounds fun.
Sometimes we scrimmage the boys' team.
They crush us every time.
We suck."

She took off her glasses and placed them on the shelf in her locker.

"Maybe you can help us not suck this year."

Our team still sucked.

But Jen and I found out we were great together
both on and off the soccer field.

Jon and I are birthday twins.
We were both born on July 18th
but he was in New York
and I was in Delaware.
We figured out that he's about five hours older.

We met in Oral Communications class in 10th grade.
We sat right next to each other.
Jon's imitation of Mrs. Bindy
made me need to stifle the uncontrolled snorts escaping my throat
while wiping black mascara tears from my cheeks.

Jon has a skaterdo
cut short in back with a long swath of bangs
that he constantly sweeps across his forehead
out of his eyes.
He's a little short for a guy—
about my height—
but he has a tall guy's personality
smart, funny, and confident.

And he's a good listener.
It's easy to tell him everything you really think
and then wonder if maybe you shouldn't have.

For our birthday
our friends throw us a party in Steve's basement.
There's a banner taped to the wall above the couch.

Happy 17th Birthday, John and Kelly!

They've misspelled both our names—
like most people do—
as a joke.

The Spoofers

is the name for our group of friends at school.
I'm not sure which of the guys made the name up.
It sounds silly and innocuous
like we are just a bunch of goofy nerds.
Actually, it refers to something sexual
as most high school jokes do.

It's hard to know exactly how many people
would call themselves a "Spoofer"
but there is a core group
who have been there since the beginning
and will stick with us
through it all this year.

Steve Yates has been Steve's best friend
since about 2nd grade.
(Often called Stevie—by the girls—or Yates, to differentiate.)
But about the only thing they have in common any more
is their taste in music.
Steve is smart and athletic and quiet.
Yates is taking Biology for the third time
gave up sports in junior high
and is the life of every party.
He is the most charming person I've ever met
and has more friends than anyone I know.
He was one of my first friends when I moved to Maryland
thanks to an introduction by Jenny
in the art class we all had together.

Brian is the politician.
He switches easily
from smart, confident, articulate, and personable
to irreverent, mischievous, and flirtatious
depending on the audience.
Somehow, he gets away with wearing aqua boat shoes
with pastel plaid pants
and playing tuba in the marching band
while remaining obstinately popular.

He's the same Brian
who first introduced me to Steve
and then later
told me to get a ride with him
after field hockey practice
which led to our first date.

Bill is hard to pin down.
I don't know him as well as the others.
He's quieter and has that still-waters-run-deep vibe.
He's anti-establishment, but not belligerent about it.
Like wearing a cutoff sweatpant leg on his head instead of a hat
and not caring what you think about it.
He's smart, funny, athletic, and very cute
but doesn't play up any of these
so it might all go unnoticed
if you don't know what to look for.

The guys call the girls "The Spoofettes".
And we let them.

Julie is the smart, ambitious one.
She will go to an Ivy League and make lots of money
like her parent's and brothers.
She's tiny and gregarious and logical and confident.
Not like me at all
except we both talk a lot.

Becky is the quirky, confident artist.
She wears bright clothes with bold prints
and rainbow eyeshadow.
She painted a mural on the side of her parents' old car
and she takes calculus and AP bio
so, an intelligent artist.

There's Jenny, of course, who the guys call "Hot Pants".
They don't mention the fact that she's smart
and crazy talented with ink and pastels.
Instead, they focus on her long, thin brown legs
drawing their eyes up to a round butt.

She seems unsure if it's a compliment or not
acting embarrassed and a little mad
even though she usually smiles.
I'm a little jealous of the attention.

And then there's Mark, the musician.
Ryan, the Canadian asshole.
Jon, my birthday buddy.
And Steve, my heart.

And me.
I don't know what role
the other Spoofers would give me.

I'm in honors English and History

                                but I'm just average in Math and Science.

I play varsity sports

                                but I'm never the star.

I'm talkative and love to socialize

                                but I don't like to take risks or get in trouble.

And growing up in Catholic schools
has left me pretty naive.

So, I guess I might be called "the goody-goody".

                    Except now
        that Steve and I have been practically inseparable
                    for almost a year
            I think most people just consider me to be
                one half of "Steve and Kelley".

            That sounds perfect to me.

We work in the dining room
at Asbury Methodist Home.
It's a home for senior citizens.
Steve, Jenny, Jon, and I wait tables.
Brian washes dishes
while throwing insults at Bill, who passes for a cook
when he doesn't burn the Jell-O.

The dinner shift is 4:00 - 7:30
which is good for after school
or 6:00 - 2:00 for the breakfast and lunch shifts
which borders on torture, to a teenager.

The girls wear a poop-brown, polyester dress
a white apron with two spacious pockets
white, rubber-soled shoes
and a hairnet.
We used to have to wear pantyhose too
but we complained because they're hot and itchy.
We badgered the managers for months.

There's no hygienic reason for it.

They cause foot fungus and yeast infections.

It's sexist.

The residents don't even notice we have legs, much less what's on them.
Take a poll as they leave the dining room and see for yourself!

Finally, they gave in
and now we can wear socks instead.

It's mostly an easy job.
A few of the old people are cranky
but most of them are sweet.
They sneak ribbons or a piece of candy into my apron pocket.
Even though we aren't allowed to accept tips or gifts
I don't refuse them.
It makes them believe they are caring for me

instead of the other way around.
Like when they used to matter.

They always sit in the same seat
at the same table
with the same friends.
It's a lot like high school.

There is a group of them who are clearly the popular kids.
Healthy
well-dressed
hair freshly salon-styled
always smiling and laughing.
They wave and call to their friends as they arrive
holding court from a big table in the center of the room.
They call me "honey" or "dear"
and scoff at the school cafeteria-style foods
on the disposable paper menu.
They leave all at once
Avon vapor trails wafting after them.

Mrs. Van Zandt is always first at the door for dinner.
She sits in the first chair
at the first table
right next to the podium
where Wanda, the manager, checks residents in
to make sure no one is missing meals.
Mrs. Van Zandt's large chest rests
on the top of the table
and is splotched with food stains from her last meal.
She is always angry
barking at her server and the tiny timid women
who are afraid to sit somewhere else.
She wears bright scarlet lipstick
turning her mouth into a loud, wrinkled scar.

Wanda hands the old woman a laminated card with a circular sticker
that's the same color as her lipstick
indicating she's diabetic.

This means she must have the canned prunes for dessert
instead of the frozen yogurt.
She tries to hide her card under the pastel paper placemat.
Sometimes, she even tricks the new servers
into bringing her the sugared treat.

Tall and broomstick-thin, Mr. Miller
marches in long strides to his table
on the far side of the room.
He sits in the chair with his back to the window
and begins to rearrange his place setting.
You think he will be mean, since no one will sit with him
but he's very polite.

> "Black coffee, please.
> That's perfect.
> Thank you."

He brings a newspaper or novel to read while he eats
and he makes fun of the "fancy ladies" who are all "stuck up"
and crazy Ms. Butler.

> "She came down for breakfast three times this morning.
> She doesn't remember she already ate!
> She's going to be as big as a barn when she dies.
> They won't be able to fit her in a coffin."

He mumbles this to me as I refill his coffee
in between quick bites of Salisbury steak
never lifting his gaze from his meal.

Mr. Miller always tells us to call him Charlie.
He's my favorite.

Steve and I
spend most of our time together
hanging out less and less
with our friends or family.

We watch tv in the basement
or go to the movies
or concerts.
We go for long walks around our neighborhoods
or nearby parks
and play mini golf or catch.
We lie on the floor in his bedroom
and listen to music.
We wander the mall
looking at shoes
skateboards
and records.
Then we get a slice of pizza
or a shake to share.

I always want him close enough to touch
our fingers loosely hooked
or his hand resting on my hip
or mine twining
through the waves of his hair against his neck.

When I'm not with him I wonder
what he is doing
who he is with
what he is thinking
when he will be with me again.

There are parts of myself
that love Steve in a way I never have before
with anyone else.
Parts that he sees
and understands.
No one and nothing else
matters to me as much.

Certainly not
my family
who loved me first.

Or God
who I'm meant to love
above all things.

Not even Jenny.

Or any of the rest of the Spoofers.

No one else makes me feel
as perfectly ME
as he does.

I was right.
This is the best summer
of my life.

AUGUST

———

I can still hear the music
coming from the house
a muffled thudding, making its way
through the glass of the storm door

down the front walk

across the parking lot

to this circular median of grass

where I'm hiding.

From Steve
Jenny
everyone.

And especially
all the work of trying to be
cool
interesting
fun
or just
normal.

I can't do it.
Not now.

Staring at the night sky
is supposed to make you feel
tiny
insignificant.

But tonight
it's the stars that seem
miniscule
almost invisible.

And I feel
IMPOSSIBLY HUGE
DENSE
like a black hole
sucking the universe into my center.

Lying on my back
I press my palms flat against my belly
pushing down.
Willing it
empty.

While wet falling stars

trace shiny trails

across my moon cheeks

and
pool
in the
craters
of my
ears.

"Kelley, where are you?"
Steve calls for me from the doorway
a porchlight halo
gilding his head and shoulders.
Glowing
like an angel
or a knight.

"Here," barely a whisper
from my tightened throat.
I lay my arm across my face as he sits beside me
hiding my red swollen eyes in the crook of my elbow.

Taking my free hand in his
he strokes my index finger with his thumb.
"Hey, Red, what's wrong?
Why are you out here in the dark?"

He thinks he can rescue me
but he doesn't know
and I don't want to tell him
that he's trapped too.

I've been holding my breath
trying to stop the sobs
threatening to vomit from my throat
but I can't bear being alone with this
any longer.

He startles at my violent exhale
and the trembling of my body.
Then, letting go of my hand
he pulls me up by the shoulders
wrapping me in his arms.

My sobs explode into the warmth of his chest.

Suddenly panicked, he pleads
"What is it? Tell me, Kelley. You're scaring me."

So I do.

And now my fears have company.

The Zeph

is his car.
It's a Ford Zephyr station wagon
pancake-batter yellow.
Room for seven
or nine
when we escape the cafeteria for KFC.

Or two.
Stretched out in the wayback.

"You okay?"
He slides the back of his open hand across the seat
palm up, fingers curled
like a question mark.

He knows I'm not
and I don't know how to answer
so I don't.

I roll the window down
and rest my temple against the doorframe.

A zephyr is also a soft breeze.
It dries my tears
crusting them to my cheeks and neck.

After he watches her walk into the house
Steve turns the stereo up louder
on the Thompson Twins album
that's playing in the tape deck.

And then again
louder still
as he pulls out of the driveway.
He tries to fill his head
with the drumbeats
the keyboard
and Tom Bailey's mournful voice.
Anybody's voice
other than hers
or his own.

He rounds the corner
and pulls to the side of the road.
He clenches his shaking hands into fists.

It's my fault, he thinks.
How could I let this happen?

"FUCK!" he screams
slamming his fists into the steering wheel.

Breathing heavily
he works to convince himself it's okay.
Maybe she's just a little late.
Maybe it will all be fine.

Steve punches the eject button on the tape deck
rips the cartridge from the slot, and violently hurls it
toward the open passenger window.
It makes a loud thunk when it hits the glass
and falls stupidly onto the seat
that is still warm with her scent.

In the morning
my bladder wakes me.

I pretend I can't hear it.
But it insists.

Traitor.

Bathroom tile is always cold
even in the summer.

My fingers tremble as I slide my underwear down.
My legs shake as my thighs touch the porcelain.

The stream slaps the water
but I feel no relief.

I just want to stop
the knowing.

Tightly squeezing my eyes and knees together
I clench the damp tissue
still white
in my fist.

"Kelley, get out! It's my turn!" my sister hollers
cold as the bathroom tile.

Mom does her ironing
in front of the tv
the board set up behind the couch
watching soap operas.
The steam shushes folds into my dad's handkerchiefs.

I curl up on the couch
pulling my knees in tight to my chest
wondering if I'm just imagining
that my nipples feel different.

"What happened?" she asks suddenly
smoothing the crease into a pair of slacks.
"Did you and Steve have sex?"

"Ha!" coughs out from my throat like a hiccup.
"If only that were the problem."

Her arm is still.
The iron, nose up, hisses a vapor cloud over her face.

"Are you late?"

"I don't know.
                    Maybe.
                              I think so."

She doesn't say anything
for a long while.

I keep my back to her and the ironing board
watching the drama on tv
which is laughable.
Not at all like real life.

But no one is laughing.

"Get dressed. We're going to the clinic," she finally says.
"And you can tell Steve to talk to his parents now
or they can find out when we get there."

Somehow no one is yelling
or crying.
And I'm not sure why not.

I'm still in my bathrobe
sitting on the vanity stool in my bedroom
staring in the mirror at my wet hair
when I call Steve.

I feel sick to my stomach as I tell him.
"My mom knows. She's taking me to the clinic. Now."

He doesn't respond, but I can hear him breathing.

I lick my lips and try to swallow past the tightness in my throat.

"And I'm supposed to tell you
that we are coming over afterwards.
You can tell your parents now or when we get there."

"Okay" is all he says.

He tells his mom
in the kitchen
where she is fixing herself a piece of toast.

He doesn't look at her face
but he knows she is shocked
and angry.

"Why couldn't you just spend
five
goddamn
dollars
for a box of condoms, Steven?"

The clinic
is even colder than our bathroom.
The air conditioning blows relentlessly from the vents
raising goose pimples on my bare arms.

It's like the Arctic. Everything is colorless and frigid.
Beige square floor tiles.
Eggshell walls.
Gray plastic chairs.
Faded PSA posters.
Stark white nurses' uniforms.
Even their clipped, efficient voices.

"Miss Dietsch?"

She mispronounces our name
like everyone does when reading it the first time.
She says it with a long I, like in "sight"
instead of a long E, like in "beach".
Neither of us corrects her.

Mom comes back with me.
Her lips are pressed together in a tight line.
Her eyes are clear and dry.

They talk about me over my head.

"What brings you here today?"

"My daughter needs a pregnancy test."

"Okay.
What is the date of her last period?"

"Late June or early July, she thinks
but she's not sure of the exact date."

"So she's only a couple of weeks late
at this point?"

"I suppose so."

"Then we will have to draw blood.
It's too soon to tell with a urine sample."

"How long will it take until we know?"

"About an hour.
We can call you at home
as soon as we have the results.
What number would you like us to call?"

"Tell her Steve's number.
We'll wait there
for the call."

It's like being underwater.
Everything is distorted and muffled.
Limbs numb and weightless.
Faces blurry.
Voices garbled.
Light piercing.

"Kelley."

Mom's voice pulls me to the surface.

"The nurse is waiting."

His mom answers the door.
I keep my eyes on her white Keds.

I feel her fingertips lift my chin
but I don't look at her until she says
"You put your head up. You didn't get into this by yourself."

Then she pulls me toward her soft body
and wraps her arms around me.

I want to collapse into her
but I can only manage to hunch my shoulders toward her a little
keeping my arms rigid at my side.

I don't deserve her compassion.

Why hasn't anybody yelled at me yet?

We sit at the kitchen table
waiting
for the phone on the wall above our heads
to ring.

Except for Steve, far away
on the edge of the couch of the adjacent family room.
We don't try to touch
or even stand in each other's view.

We all sit awkwardly and anxiously.

Wordlessly, Steve and I seem to agree
that sitting close or touching in any way
would be viewed with disgust by our mothers—
a rudely obnoxious gesture
echoing the immature and careless behavior
that precipitated this potential catastrophe.

I'd sooner slap my mom in the face
than reach for Steve's hand in this moment.

I don't notice if our mothers speak
only the clenching in my stomach and the thudding of my heart.
My eyes fix on a placemat on the table.
Large pink and white flowers
blooming on intertwining vines
against a field of blue.

I clasp my cold hands tightly in my lap under the table.
A wordless desperate prayer.

Then the phone rings.

Everyone looks at me.

I feel my heart punching my stomach
and echoing in my eardrums.

I stand and lift the handle.

"Hello?"

"Yes."

> I don't know what she says, but I am
> crumbling
> heaving
> sinking.
> My body feels dizzyingly vaporous.
> And I desperately hope to disappear
> into the air.

The phone is gently pried from my grasp.
My mother's voice is polite, emotionless.

"Hello? This is her mother."

"No, not right now."

"Thank you. Goodbye."

I hear the receiver click into the cradle when she hangs up.

The front door slams.

My mom has her arm around me
and she is guiding me to the couch
as sobs contort my body.
I can't catch my breath
and I can't see.

I'm sorry.
I'm sorry.
I'm sorry.
I'm sorry.

I chant over and over
but maybe not out loud.

She rocks me and rubs my back
and wipes my hair away from my wet, snotty face.

I'm sorry.
I'm sorry.
I'm sorry.
I'm sorry.

She doesn't say anything.
She doesn't even cry.

Where is he?
I sit up and look around the room
suck in air
and hold it.

He's not here.

I realize I'm standing now
and my mom is looking out the sliding glass door
behind the kitchen table.

I find him
sitting on the top of the hill behind his house
where he sometimes hits the tennis ball
to his dog Maxi.

He's clutching the top of his head with both hands
pulling it down between his knees
like he's holding himself underwater
and he's rocking
back
and
forth.
His mother sits beside him
a hand resting between his shoulders.

I catch glimpses of his scrunched face
and I hear his cries
like short
strangled
coughs.
It scares me.

I suddenly stop crying myself
and slowly climb the hill
almost afraid to see his pain up close.
I fall on my knees in front of his feet
like I'm genuflecting.
A silent, humble offering.
He doesn't look at me.

He just reaches out
pulling me to him
and lowers his face onto my chest
clasping his arms around my waist
like a little boy.

I drop my forehead onto his shoulder
and we cry together.

She told him.
She said she wouldn't.
Not for a while.
But I know he knows
the moment he walks into my bedroom
after two quick taps on the door.

Steve and I quickly sit up on my bed
and move away from each other.
Steve swings his feet to the floor.

My dad doesn't even look at us
until he is leaning against my dresser at the foot of my bed
arms crossed over his chest.
I notice his eyes are red-rimmed
as he wipes his hand over his mouth
and swallows loudly.

Steve and I sit frozen
afraid to even rustle the blankets, waiting.

Then he points at Steve and spouts
"Can't you keep your cock in your fucking pants?"

My mother wastes no time
in a crisis.

Within a week
we have an appointment at the school
to meet with a counselor.

Mr. Tolbert is tall and very thin.
You can tell he is a runner
even when he wears a tie.
His smile is wide, reaching his eyes
as he holds out his hand to shake my mother's
and then mine.

My mom explains to him my problem.
He nods seriously, his smile fading
to something appropriately grim.

As he looks through my file he says
"It seems you only really need one more English credit
to graduate.
You could take two English classes the first semester
and graduate in December."

"I want to graduate with my class.
In June," I say.

"Well, you can't be a student here
without taking classes in the spring."

"Don't some students take college classes?"

"Yes, that's possible.
Do you have at least a 2.5 GPA?"
He scans my file.

"I have a 3.5."

He raises his eyebrows in surprise.

He thinks I must be an irresponsible and careless student too
to get myself in this situation.

"Well then, I'm sure we can make that work."
Mr. Tolbert smiles again, closing my file.

Then he adds, "The nurse must be informed
about all pregnant students in the school
you understand?"

Fine.
Whatever.

As Steve approaches the front door
he notices it is already open.
Then her father steps out onto the porch.
Steve hasn't seen him since that day in Kelley's bedroom.

The boy comes to an abrupt standstill, mid-stride
paralyzed
in the middle of the walkway
for a few skittery heartbeats.

Then, with a single exhale
his body trembles awake as if by an electric shock.
Anxiously, Steve stuffs his hands in his pockets
squeezing them into fists.
Hunching his shoulders toward his ears
he ducks his head and locks his eyes on the gap
between the stones under his feet.
In a moment he has transformed
from a hale and hopeful young man
to a nervous, naughty child.

Mr. Dietsch leaves the door open and walks to the edge of the step.
His eyes are angry slits
and his jaw is clenched, muscles twitching in his cheeks.
His face is a placard of contempt.

"I don't want you here," he growls.

Feeling suddenly that he might vomit
Steve quickly turns and fumbles in his pocket for his keys.

How could he have believed his own lies?
he wonders.
Everything is NOT going to be okay.
He WON'T get past this.
EVERYONE does not make mistakes, not like THIS one.

As he hurries back to his car
Steve hears her father raise his stern voice to add
"No matter what, this baby will always be a Dietsch!"

August 25, 1987

10:23 pm

Dear Steve,

I can't believe it's only been four days since you left. It feels like months. I don't think we've gone this long without talking since we've been together.

Every time the phone rings, I hope it's you. I hate answering it because of the sick feeling I get when it's not your voice.

I'm trying to keep busy. Yesterday I made cookies with Mom, Aunt Donna, and Gramma. Mom asked me if I'd gotten any letters from you. When I said no, she said, "See, he's forgotten you already!"

That's not true, is it?

Why did you agree to go to your aunt and uncle's? I never would have given in, but you did, and now you won't even call. Are you trying to remember what it's like to not be with me all the time?

Everyone says the guy will leave. Is that what's happening? I think that's what your parents want. Why should they let this ruin two lives?

Today we went to Harper's Ferry for the day. I took a lot of pictures with Dad's camera. It was fun thinking about lives long ago instead of mine. It was really hot, and I started to feel a little queasy. It's like if I don't eat the moment I feel hungry then it's too late, and then I can't eat anything without bringing it right back up.

Mom started teasing me about being moody to make Gramma laugh, "She gets like a bear every other week and we just throw food at her."

Gramma did laugh, but then she said, "I bet only when Steve's gone."

Which impressed me. I had no idea she was so perceptive.

Please call me.

I love you.

Kelley

Inside the envelope
there is only a skinny newspaper clipping of a single headline
from Harrisburg's *The Evening News.*

"Stevie Smith Continues to Make Auto Racing Waves"

In the margin in red felt-tip ink
he has scrawled a short note.

I've been keeping busy.
See, I am the best driver!
Love, Stevie

I laugh out loud
and quickly swipe away tears of relief.

SEPTEMBER

———

How do you grieve
the loss of something
when you never really had it anyway
it's your fault it's lost
and it's a secret?

You tell yourself that you don't deserve to
and you can't afford to.

And then maybe
the unspent grief poisons you
a little bit each day.
And your body will just keep trying to spit it out.
Anyway it can.

For the first day of school

I wear a navy blue tank top
tucked into a new pair of thin pinstriped, cotton pants
pegged at the ankles
and matching navy blue Keds.

I smooth the sides of my hair back from my face
and tie the pieces in place with a white scrunchie.
I look the same as usual
except maybe a little paler
which is because I had to get up so early.

The nausea isn't as bad if I can sleep in.

I try nibbling Saltines that Mom gave me
and sipping water
but I only feel worse.
I don't want to brush my teeth
because I'll gag on my toothbrush.

Upstairs
Mom has started our back-to-school breakfast.
Suddenly I get a whiff of the eggs and bacon
curling under the crack of the bathroom door.
Clammy sweat prickles along my hairline
and saliva fills my mouth.
My stomach heaves upward
and I drop to the tile floor in front of the toilet
clutching my hair at the back of my neck
to keep it out of the way of the vomit.

I spit what's left of the paste
of crackers and water from my mouth
and grab some toilet paper to wipe my nose and lips
and the tears that have been forced from my eyes.

I hate throwing up, but now I can brush my teeth.

I pick Steve up in the Beach-mobile
around 7:00.

(The Zeph died at the end of the summer.
RIP, old friend.)

I ask him to drive
in case we have to pull over
so I can throw up again.

When we get to the parking lot
of Gaithersburg High School, it is almost full.
Not just with cars
but with the whole upper class student body
staking boundary lines and claiming allies.

We find the corner of the lot
with Jon's tiny pale blue Triumph
Jenny's beat up Datsun
Bill's tan colored Civic
otherwise known as the Muscle Machine
and Becky's old Chrysler
with its colorful mural painted down the side.

Each car spills out two or three more grinning teenagers
with summer-browned skin
freshly blown-dry hairstyles
and carefully crafted fashion statements.

We approach the school building en masse
pushing through the crowd toward the main entrance
and parting the throng of underclassmen
who are debussing onto the wide circular sidewalk.

We are The Senior Class of 1988
and this is our school.
We plan to leave our mark on it
before we leave.

Steve and I trail a little behind the crowd.

I clasp his hand tightly in mine
trying to quell the ever-present nausea
which at this moment
may not actually be the result of morning sickness.

SCHOOL: Gaithersburg High   **SEMESTER:** Fall 1988
STUDENT: Dietsch Kelley M   **STUDENT ID:** 536833
GRADE: 12   **COUNSELOR:** Tolbert H

PERIOD 1: Problems of the 20th Century   **TEACHER:** Adams

> He lives four doors up from my house
> and is a friend of my parents.
> Like, they go over to his house for dinner parties.
> Totally weird.

Steve, Brian, Julie, Jim, Jon, Bill, Susan
and maybe a few more, are all in this class too.
Of course it isn't a coincidence.
We plan these things.

PERIOD 2: Advanced Composition   **TEACHER:** Cernak/Shanks

> A co-teaching experiment of some sort, I guess?
> Maybe they're best friends. Or lesbian lovers.
> Whatever.

With Steve again. Of course.
He's really good at creative writing: stories, song lyrics, poetry.
I suck at it, but I'm competitive.
Can't let him get a better grade than me!

PERIOD 3: Introduction to Business   **TEACHER:** Bowman

> Never heard of her.

An elective with no one I know
to fill the hole in my schedule.
Could be useful for college.

PERIOD 4: Essay and Lyric   **TEACHER:** Scanlon

This is my extra English credit
that I need to graduate.

> They say he's an asshole, but
> Steve's in this class, so
> I picked this section on purpose.
> Study buddy!

PERIOD 5: LUNCH!

With Steve and a few other Spoofers
preferably spent at KFC or Burger King
rather than the cafeteria.

PERIOD 6: Trigonometry   **TEACHER:** Diamandis

> Also the girls' basketball coach
> who keeps trying to recruit me
> for some reason.
> I'm not even tall.

Jenny and I have had math together since 9th grade.
Math is not my thing.
Steve will try to help me, but
teaching is not his thing.

PERIOD 7: Advanced Placement English   **TEACHER:** Sampselle

THIS is my thing.

> Coolest teacher ever, even if
> I can't get higher than a B+ in his class.
> I had him junior year too
> and he always let me down softly
> by grading all my essays in pencil.

PERIOD 8: Advanced Placement Physics   **TEACHER:** Roe

> **DOCTOR** Roe, that is.
> Classic absent-minded professor.
> Meaning he's brilliant, but I will learn
> almost nothing.

What was I thinking?!
Steve promised to get me through this
even though
I haven't mastered the necessary math.
I'm doomed.

Business class
is in E hall in the back corner of the building.
It's where all computer and typing classes are located.
More outlets there, I suppose.

Steve's class is at the opposite end of the building though
so we split ways.
After having spent the first two periods of the day together
for some reason I'm nervous on my own.
It's like being a freshman all over again.
I won't know anyone in this class
and I'll have to find a seat that tells everyone
what type of person I am.

Not the middle of the back rows
which is for those who don't give a shit
vocally
as a group.

Or the far back corners
for those who don't give a shit either
but in an isolated-loner way.

And not too presumptuous
like the center of the room
reserved for the confident, popular people
and their best friends.

Or too nerdy
like in the front row right under the teacher's chin
for the confidently unpopular people
who have no friends
and pretend to like it that way.

Somewhere near the middle
so people know that I'm a good student.
But more off to one side
so I don't look like a wannabe.

But when I finally arrive

about 30 seconds before the six-minute passing bell goes off
there isn't much of a choice left.
A quick perusal of the room
confirms what I expected.
I don't know anyone.

Well, I know *of*
several someones, but only by name.
I've never spoken to any of them before
or they to me.

There are actually tables in the room, instead of desks
so I'll have to share a space with someone.
All the someones with an available neighboring chair
are carefully not making eye contact with me
and I've already stood too long at the door.
A few seconds longer and eyes will start to rest on me
with either contempt
or amusement.
I drop my purse on the table closest to the door
which happens to still have both chairs open
leaving my neighbor up to fate.

I begin to look through my purse for a pen
when another girl appears in the doorway
walks behind my chair
and then turns and sits right next to me.
Her name is Patti...
Something.
She usually hangs with the Vo-Tech kids
who spend study hall and lunch periods
in the courtyard smoking section.

She's pretty
in a hard sort of way.
She's all sharp angles.
Her hair is shaved
very short around her neck and ears
and bleached Madonna-blond.
Her bangs are slightly longer

and teased up high from her forehead
into a hairy jersey wall
that separates her face from her scalp.
They are frozen in place with a layer of Aqua Net
which, I gather from the residual fumes
was just reapplied
moments before she arrived.

She has startling blue eyes
that are rimmed with a thick line of glittery turquoise pencil.
Shimmery rose-colored powder
is smoothed over her eyelids and her high, sharp cheekbones.
Her lips are pink and glossy, the same color of the gum
that she blows into a bubble the size of a baseball
and then swallows whole
popping it loudly inside her cheek.
She has a half-dozen silver and rhinestone studs
lining the cartilage all the way up the edge of her ear
to its tip
and a fist-sized silver hoop swinging
from the lowest hole in her lobe.

She doesn't even glance my way
before busily digging into her purse.
I assume she's looking for a pen
but with so much stuffed in the tiny leather bag
the size of a greeting card envelope
she can't seem to locate one.
Finally, she simply upends it
and dumps everything onto the table.

By this time, Mrs. Bowman has started taking attendance.
My last name beginning with a D
I'm called early in the list
and, after declaring my presence
I return my attention to Patti out of the corner of my eye
trying not to appear like I'm watching her.

I'm just about to offer her one of my extra pens
when I notice that her lip gloss

is rolling toward the edge of the table.
Both of us lunge for it at the same time, but only succeed
in pushing it the last inch over the edge.

"Shit," Patti whispers
as she pushes back her chair and stands up.

Now that she is standing directly in front of me
I only just notice
that Patti's bright floral blouse is tented out in front of her
like a sloped shelf.

She must be at least six months pregnant!

I freeze
staring at her waist.
My heart is suddenly pounding frantically
and I feel dizzy.

Patti slowly walks around to the front of the table
and awkwardly bends over
to retrieve her tube of lip gloss.
Just as she stands up again, Mrs. Bowman calls her name.

"Patricia?"

Without so much as a glance in the teacher's direction
the girl drops back onto her chair
with a small puff of air, and loudly yells
"It's Patti. I go by Patti. With an i."
Then she opens the lip gloss
and runs the pink contoured sponge over her pouty bottom lip.
She massages both lips together
smoothing the color perfectly in place.
Screwing the brush back into the tube
she returns to sorting the contents of her purse
never once looking
at me, Mrs. Bowman, or anyone else in the room.

I'm starting to feel hot and queasy and raise my hand
to ask to be excused.

At Mrs. Bowman's nod, I gather my purse and notebooks
and slip quickly out of the room
heading directly to Mr. Tolbert's office.

I need to change my schedule.
NOW.

All day
in every class
all I think about
is my huge secret.

How if I'm found out
everything will be different.

I'll be an outcast.
I'll have no friends.
Who invites a pregnant girl to a party?
Or to shop at the mall?
Or to a sleepover?

Their parents will use me as a warning.
Look what happens
when you sneak around and break the rules.
No college.
No career.
No nice car.
No cool apartment in the city.
No traveling to see the world.
No life.

And the teachers will write me off
as another sad case
of lost potential.
They'll be surprised to realize I am one of
those kind of girls.
More into parties than planning for my future.
Why take AP English
if you're going to wind up working at the A&P
as a cashier?

I'm on guard and tense
all day.

Trying to disguise
the slight expansion of my waist
with big sweaters over leggings.

Breathing through my mouth in the cafeteria
sickened by the hot meat smells.

Trying to focus
on Melville
and the Russian Revolution
and cosines.

It's exhausting.
Pretending.
And hiding.

All day.

Every day.

Day after day.

Field hockey practice
is the only time of day when I feel like myself.

I try to be early or late to the locker room
so I can miss Julie and Susan and change alone.
They've joined the JV team
so they can put athletics on their college applications
and look "well-rounded."

That term makes me feel a little bit hysterical.
I bite my lip
to keep a giggle from escaping.
The last thing I want people to notice about me right now
is that I'm becoming
more rounded.
I've already had to exchange my uniform skirt
for a larger size.

I work hard at practice.
Sprinting
up the field until I'm huffing breathlessly.
Racing
an opponent to be there first.
Swinging
my stick violently.
Battling
for ownership of the ball.

Several of my teammates are more skilled than me
but no one plays with more hustle or aggression.

I'm not trying to impress the coach
or even become a better player.
I just want to be too hot and tired to think.
For a couple of hours, I can rage at something
other than myself.

I feel strong.
Powerful.
In control.

I leave the field with a broad smile
my face flushed and sweaty.
Strands of hair from my ponytail cling wetly to my neck.
Resting my stick on my shoulder, I sigh
with the pleasure of tired muscles
and the relief of realizing
I don't feel my stomach
at this moment.

Steve waits for me on the bleachers
and walks me to the doors of the locker room.
He hands me his can of Orange Crush.
He'll wait until I come out and walk with me to the car.
I'll drop him off at home before heading to mine.

He could get a ride home with Bill or Jon
but it would mean we wouldn't see each other
until tomorrow morning
when I'll be sick and stressed
all over again.

After practice I'm my old self
relaxed
cheerful
carefree
for a little while.

I don't ask him to stay.
He just knows, and does.

Family counseling
sounds like a good idea, given our situation.

Me with my parents
and Steve with his
are all going together.

Four against two
feels incredibly unfair and scary.

Joe Tooley, the counselor
is relaxed and friendly.
He has dark hair, a dark beard
and tortoiseshell-rimmed glasses.
He wears a plaid shirt and jeans.
He welcomes me with a smile and a handshake
and tells us to call him "Joe".

He gestures toward a stark sitting area
that looks like a monk's cell.
Empty white walls
and brown pillowless chairs and sofas.
Steve and I sit together on the loveseat.

I'm not sure what to expect.

Do they want to know
what my plans are?

                                    Because I don't have any
                                                    yet.

Do they want to tell me
what they think I should do?

                                    I'm not sure that I need
                                              or want
                                         to know that.

Maybe they just want a chance
to tell us how they feel.

I suppose
we owe them that.

Could Steve have something he wants
to tell me and is afraid to do it alone?

God, no.

Turns out, Steve and I don't say hardly anything
because we don't have much to say.

Yes, we agree, we totally fucked up.
And no, we have no idea what we're going to do about it.
That about sums up our side of things at this point.

Joe basically reviews the three options we have
which I suppose we already know but haven't said out loud.

Abortion
Adoption
Parenting

My mother shares that they cannot
in good conscience
pay for or take me to get an abortion
but will not prevent me from doing so, if that's what I decide to do
since I'm "obviously already making adult decisions".

But we aren't. Not really.
We never made a decision to get pregnant.
Or even to have sex.
It just happened.
But neither of us say that, or anything else.
We just sit, still and silent.
Like the couch cushions.

Sex was another secret
Steve and I kept.
Something that we didn't talk about
even to each other.

I was taught sex was for married couples
to make babies.
It's private and mysterious
and always a little naughty.

My mother gave me the clinical explanation when I was eight
because Anjanette Willis told me
a boy sticks his wiener into a girl
which I thought was a nasty lie.

I learned from my mom that Anjanette was essentially right
even if I couldn't imagine
the positions a couple must contort themselves into
to get that floppy worm to penetrate a woman
like a vaccination delivering its magical seed.

In 8th grade
I had a Catholics school's version of sex education
provided by a classmate's nurse-mother.
It included brand new words
like "masturbation" and "orgasm"
but wasn't any more enlightening
than my earlier bewildering instruction.
Her euphemistic explanations left me more confused
and curious
than ever before.

So when I fell in love at sixteen
I didn't really understand that sex is both
the emotional and the physical
inextricably enmeshed.

It was all a secret.
I couldn't talk to anyone.
Not my older sister

or my girlfriends
and definitely not my mother.
When it became obvious to me that I couldn't
wouldn't
say no to Steve anymore
my lust-logical conclusion
was to give in to the constant lure of sex
but reject "artificial" birth control.

I was doing one bad thing; why make it worse
by doing two?

We tried to prevent conception "naturally"
which any parent will tell you does not work.
But we were naive and horny enough to think it would.

This mixed-up mess of sexual awakening
resulted in such reticent and tense lovemaking
that I can't even tell you
precisely
which encounter ended in the loss of our shared virginity.

It was all a secret.
Even to us.

Steve's parents drive us to a park.
It's clear we will not be picnicking or hiking the trails.
We are here for neutral ground and privacy.

We wander a ways from the parking lot
and find a picnic table under a tree.
Mrs. Smith sits down on the bench, and I follow her lead
sitting on the other bench on the opposite end
putting the table's width and length between us.
Steve walks behind me, and leans against the tree
while Mr. Smith remains standing, facing us all.

It's obvious that he will say the first words.
We sit
still and patient
as he works to compose what he wants to say.
None of us looks at the others.

I focus on my folded hands on the table
and notice an ant
trying to navigate the crack between two planks
having no idea how far this chasm cuts through its world.
I feel sorry for it.
The distance is so much farther than it can see
or imagine
from its tiny perspective.

"Your mother and I brought you here today to talk to you
about your plans for the future," Mr. Smith finally begins.

Then turning in my direction, he continues
"Steve tells us you haven't made a decision yet
and we think it's good that you are thinking about this carefully.
It's a decision that will affect you both for the rest of your lives
and we just want to make sure that you have what you need
to do what's best for everyone involved."

I can feel the scarlet letter begin to smolder on my chest.
Involuntarily, I hunch my shoulders a little bit to hide it.
I see the ant still scurrying along the edge of the gap

its antenna feverishly twitching and searching for escape.

"Kelley, we understand
that your parents may only support the choice of an adoption
which of course is an important option
that you will be considering."

At this, I turn and look at Steve behind me
but he's not looking at me
or his dad
or at anything I can see.
He's just staring off into the distance
arms crossed over his chest.

Has he talked to his parents about adoption?
He's never mentioned it to me.
We actually haven't talked about our future at all.
We just keep trying to get through each day
each moment
to the next one.

I can't find the ant anymore.
Has it made it to the end of the table?
Did it find a way to cross the gap
or has it finally plunged blindly into the space
hopeful that it will find a way?

It's hard to think about this idea of the baby
as something real.
It's not that I don't believe it; it's just that I can't fathom it.
It's an abstract idea, like dying.
I know my life will end one day
but right now it seems really far away
and there's a lot of living to do in the meantime.

I'm just trying to deal with making it to school in the morning
and through all my classes
without throwing up on my desk
and keeping straight all the little lies I tell
my teachers

coaches
and friends
because when they know
then it will be real.

I realize
that just because Steve hasn't talked to me
about putting the baby up for adoption
doesn't mean he hasn't talked with his parents about it.
Is that what he wants?

"But there is another option too," Mr. Smith adds.
"We want you to know
that if you want to end this pregnancy
we will pay for it."

Now I turn and look directly at Steve's dad.
He is looking at his shoes
while scuffing the tip of his sneaker in the dirt.
His face is flushed.

Then I look at Mrs. Smith
but she isn't making eye contact with me either.
Her hands are resting on her thighs
and she is looking toward her husband too
but not at him, at the space behind him.

Then she says
"We think you should have all the options available to you.
We're not saying that we think you should end the pregnancy
but we want you to have the choice."

Finally, I turn on the bench to see how Steve is taking this.
He remains silent, but he too
is now looking at his shoes.

I turn my gaze back
to the rough and splintering wood of the tabletop.

Did he know

they were going to offer to pay for an abortion?
Have they talked about this before bringing me here?
That's the way it feels.
Like this is a plan they've made
to offer all of us a way out
and now they are all holding their breath
waiting to see if I will accept their offer
so we can all go back to normal.

Suddenly I notice the ant again
running up and down a different gap between the planks.
Or maybe it's a new ant with the same problem.
I place the tip of my finger on top of it
trapping it in place.

"No," I say abruptly. "I couldn't do that."

I haven't even thought about it
before this moment.

True, I was raised in a devout Catholic family
but obviously that didn't prevent me from having sex with Steve
so I can't say it is my religious beliefs
that cause me to recoil at the suggestion.
Maybe it is having grown up
in a house full of younger brothers and sisters
or just the thought of the cold surgical procedure
that terrifies me.

But it is suddenly, perfectly clear.
I am going to have this baby.

I keep my back to Steve and my eyes on the tabletop.
I lift my finger, freeing the ant.
Its tiny body trembles a moment
and then it continues its journey
still searching for a bridge across the space.

"Did you know?"
I ask him later that night on the phone.
"Did you know they were going to offer to pay
for an abortion?"

"No!" Steve answers forcefully, "I didn't."

"But do you want me to?"
I pull the mouthpiece below my chin
hoping he doesn't hear my breath quickening.
I want him to answer honestly
but I'm afraid of what he will say.

"I just want you. I want what you want."

"Steve, you have to figure out what you want."
I'm exasperated now.
"Don't make me decide all by myself."

"I don't know."
He sounds like someone is sitting on his chest.
"I'm sorry."

Then we just sit in silence.
Breathing into the space between us.

The next time
we go to Joe Tooley's office
it's just Steve and me and his parents.
He wants to talk with just the two of us
alone, first.

He asks us about what our plans were for the future
if this hadn't happened.
College?
Careers?
Lifestyle?

Then he asks us
who will watch the baby when we are at school?
How will we earn money to pay for daycare?
Where will we live?

We haven't thought about any of this yet.

I think maybe that is Tooley's point.

Then Steve's parents join us.
He asks them if they have anything they want to say to us.

They do.

They tell us that they are uncomfortable
with our behavior around their house.
They don't think we should be making out
on the couch in the family room
because it's disrespectful.

WHAT?!

I am repelled. And disgusted.
I feel my face flush in humiliation.

They have made cuddling together
under an afghan to watch a movie
something salacious.

I leave feeling like I need to take a shower.
I know that therapy is supposed to be hard work
and not just about making me feel good
but I'm also pretty sure
it's not supposed to make me feel dirty either.

Later that week, Joe Tooley calls me at home.
He tells me that he thinks Steve and I are not ready to raise a child.
He thinks we should give the baby up for adoption.

I am stunned. And furious.

I know he's broken the rules.
My mom is a counselor, and I know
he's not supposed to tell me what to do.
He's supposed to help me "consider my options."

I tell him this. And that I'm done with counseling.

Next time
Steve's parents go by themselves.

OCTOBER

———

St. Jude

is the patron Saint of desperate cases
and lost causes.
If you pray to St. Jude, and he answers your prayer
you are supposed to thank him
by printing a notification
in the classified section of the newspaper.

Prayers answered by St. Jude.

One night
while I'm leaning against the vanity in my parents' bathroom
watching my mother wash and moisturize her face
she begins to talk to me about St. Jude
and the miracles that have been attributed to him
by the hopeless and devoted.
She walks over to the tall narrow chest
in the corner of the bathroom which holds her jewelry
and takes from it a prayer card
and hands it to me.

St. Jude, glorious Apostle,
Patron of things despaired of,
Pray for me, who am so miserable.
Pray for me,
That finally I may receive
The consolations and the succor
Of Heaven in all my necessities,
Tribulations, and sufferings,
Particularly (Here make your request),
And that I may bless God
With the Elect
Throughout Eternity
Amen
St Jude Apostle, intercede for us.

"Miscarriages happen all the time in the first trimester," she says.

Then I understand what she is asking me to do.
Instantly horrified

I quickly drop the card down on the vanity
as if it is poisonous
and step back, my arms crossing over my midsection.

"I can't do that!"

I don't know why I feel so protective of this being
that doesn't even feel completely real.
So far, I've done everything I can do to deny its existence
to myself
and anyone else who might suspect.
My only feelings toward it are shame and fear.
Would it really be so bad if it all went away
after saying a few prayers?

Somehow the easy way out doesn't seem like the right way.

"I'm sorry," my mom says
and folds me into her arms.
"I'm just so worried for you.
I don't know what else to do."

It feels so good
to be held
accepted
loved
despite it all being my fault.
But it's a little scary too
because now I know
my mom feels as frightened and desperate
as I do.

At the hospital
I am a number, not a name.
All dependents of military personnel
are issued a number for identification.
I'm 02, for second dependent
plus the nine digits of my dad's social security number.
I record the number on the clipboard and sit down to wait.

Bethesda Naval Hospital is a tall white monolith
standing sentinel just inside the Washington, D.C. beltway.
Even though my dad is retired from the Air Force
we will always be a military family
so we don't have our own family doctor.
I will have my first GYN appointment
with whichever doctor is on duty today.

When they call my number, I stand up and look at my mom.
She just nods and turns back to her magazine.
This is another consequence of "adult decisions"
I suppose.

The halls are long and white, and the walls are bare
except for a few faded posters.
The nurse stops at a scale
and records my weight and height in a folder.
Then she hands me a small plastic cup
and an alcohol wipe in a paper square.

"Wait here to get a urine sample," are the first words
she says to me
and points to a line of four or five women
leaning against the wall along the hallway
outside of a door that I assume leads to the toilet.
It feels like I'm in elementary school
when the whole class took a "bathroom trip" at the same time
girls lined up on one wall, boys on the other.

When I'm through, I place the cup labeled with my number
on a metal counter in front of a large open window
lined up next to all the others.

It joins a small collection of them, looking ridiculously
like a lemonade stand.
The lab worker manning the window points a gloved hand
further down the hall to yet another doorway.

Inside, it is less like a room
than a weigh station for trucks along the highway
an off-ramp checkpoint for blood samples and pressure screenings.
I take my place at the end of the bench
that runs along the length of the back wall, scooching down
as each woman merges back out onto the prenatal parkway.

Finally, I am led into a tiny exam room
bare except for a white cabinet with a pink countertop
a turquoise plastic chair
and a pink, vinyl-cushioned table on wheels.
The nurse pulls out a drawer in the cabinet
and hands me a cloth hospital gown that was once probably white
but is now closer to beige, with tiny pink triangles on it.

"Take everything off and put this on.
The doctor will be with you in a few minutes."

I sit with my bare legs swinging over the side of the table
the white tissue paper crinkling loudly under my butt.
I hug my arms around me for warmth
and modesty.

I'm nervous about the exam.
No one has ever looked at my vagina.
Not Steve.
Not even me.

When the doctor arrives, he is very efficient
in both his words and his actions.
In no time, I am lying flat on my back
with my knees pointed to the ceiling and my feet
in cold, metal stirrups that fold out from the corners of the table.

"Scoot your buttocks down to the edge," the nurse directs.

The doctor gently presses on my thighs with his gloved hands
pushing them open.
I wish I'd left my socks on.
I wouldn't feel so exposed, and maybe
it would keep me warm enough to prevent the trembling.

Less than ten minutes later
I am once again seated upright on the table
trying to look like a strange man pushing his fingers into me
and manipulating my breasts
is normal and expected.
A doctor's exam is always a little embarrassing, but this
feels like a violation
or an assault.

I try to listen to what the doctor is saying
tightly clutching my arms around my body to stop the shaking.
He speaks more to the nurse than to me
who reads the data from my chart to him.
Everything is normal, at least to them.

I can't name the first day of my last menstrual cycle
with any real accuracy.

Sometime in late June or early July, maybe?
I definitely didn't have it on July 4th.
We were on the mall in D.C. to see the fireworks
I remember
the lines at the porta potty were dozens of people long
so I waited, in bladder-bulging pain, until I got home.

This seems to be just one more example of my careless immaturity
from the look on the nurse's face.
She declares my due date to be April 12th, or thereabout.

The doctor, whose name I still do not know
tells me I need to gain some weight.
I couldn't even if I wanted to
since only one meal a day stays in my stomach.

He prescribes a slew of pills—
prenatal vitamins
iron tablets
and anti-nausea medication, via suppository.
This may be a case of the cure being worse than the disease.

Finally he asks me if I have any questions.

"Can I play field hockey?"

"Oh no, you shouldn't do that.
What if a ball hits you in the abdomen?"

He wants me to quit
*the **one** thing*
that still feels good in my day?!

I nod mutely
and decide immediately
that I will ignore his advice.

I can't believe I have to do this again next month.

Mr. Adams

sits on a stool behind a lab table at the front of the class
sucking on a lollipop while he takes the roll.
(He's trying to quit smoking.)

I've managed to make it to my first class on time today.
Just barely.
But I'm not going to be here for long
because I'm about to puke.
Again.

Sometimes I think this is God's way of punishing me
because he knows how much I hate to throw up
so he plans to make me do just that.
Every day.
For the entire nine months.

I'm so tired of feeling
my bruised and tender stomach all day.
I can't forget it is there.
I never realized what a blessing it is
to not feel
all the parts of your body
all the time.

Sitting next to me, Steve looks almost as pale as me
from the guilt, I think.
He knows how miserable I am and tries to comfort me
by gently stroking my back
as I cradle my head in the pillow of my arms resting on the table.
I shrug him off.
I don't want to be touched.

I raise my hand and ask to go to the bathroom.

After heaving bile and saliva into the toilet
I ask Mr. Adams for a pass to the nurse.
I haven't been to see her yet, even though Mr. Tolbert said
she is supposed to be "informed of my condition".
I don't know if he informed her, but I suppose I'm about to find out.

"I just need to lie down for a while"

I tell the nurse. "I'm sick to my stomach."

She's wearing blue scrubs
with a name tag over her heart that says "Mrs. Veazy".
She points to a paper-covered cot across the room.

"I'll be right with you," she says.

I gratefully curl up in a ball on my side and close my eyes
trying to stay as still as possible.
If I can just sleep for an hour, I'll be okay.

I open my eyes when I feel a hand on my shoulder.
It's the nurse again.
"Do you know why your stomach is upset?" she asks.

"Yes. I'm pregnant," I answer bluntly.

"I see," she says and then disappears.

I close my eyes again and hope she will leave me alone now.

A few moments later, I hear metal scraping across the tile floor
that doesn't quiet until it lands right under my head.
I open one eye and see Mrs. Veazy has pulled up a chair
and settled a few inches from my face
with a clipboard on her lap.

She adjusts her red glasses on her nose and pulls out a pen
from behind her ear.
Her blond hair is cut short in the back, but her bangs are long
and she smooths their swoop across the top of her forehead.
She is obviously a fan of Sally Jessy Raphael.

She begins to ask me a list of questions
that I respond to
with as few syllables as possible.

"Do you know how far along you are?"

"About 2 ½ months."

                              "Do your parents know?"

"Yes."

                              "Do you know who the father is?"

"Yes."

                              "Does he know that you are pregnant?"

"Yes. And so do his parents."

                              "Is he a student here too?"

"Yes."

                              "Have you seen a doctor?"

"Yes."

She is taking notes, checking off items
on what must be the "When a Student is Pregnant" form.
I have kept my eyes closed throughout the interview
swallowing the saliva filling my mouth
in between answers.

"Can't I just sleep here awhile?" I plead.
"If I sleep a bit, I'll be okay.
I really don't need anything else.
I'm fine."

                              "Yes, you can rest here some today
                    but I do need to talk to you more about this.
            I have to make sure that you have the support you need
                                          to deal with this.
                        We will have to make an appointment
          for me to come visit your home and meet your family."

- 103 -

"Really, I'm okay. Everything is fine.
I just need a nap," I insist.

"I'll give your parents a call
and set something up," she says.

I close my eyes again.

Why can't she just leave me alone?
I don't need or want her help.
I'm just a checklist to her.
A statistic.
She thinks she knows me.

She doesn't know anything.

Today I fell asleep after hockey practice
and slept through dinner.
I haven't done that since I was seven
when I spent the whole day swimming
in my neighbor's new pool.

When I finally wake up, I feel disoriented
in my dark bedroom.
I swivel my head slowly, confused
like emerging from anesthesia.

The red numbers on my clock radio glow 8:43.

I stumble heavily from my room
into the kitchen, looking for where all the humans are
and a glass of water.

"Hello," says my mom
sorting through a pile of mail on the countertop.
"Hungry?"

"I'm sorry," I croak from my dry throat.
"I can't believe I slept through dinner."

She smiles at me tenderly.
"Growing a human is exhausting."

The church is dark and quiet.
There are only a few other people in the sanctuary
kneeling in prayer.
A single candle flickers, hovering
above the tabernacle behind the altar.

My father asked me to go to confession
and I said I would
because I thought it would bring him some comfort
even if it does the opposite for me.

I slip silently into the last pew
and kneeling, bow my head, trying to gather the courage
to enter the confessional and face the priest
with a lie.

I don't really know if I can say the words
I'm meant to say
because even though I know
that the priest believes it is a sin
I can't honestly say that I regret loving Steve as I have.
But lying to a priest during the sacrament
might be worse
than not confessing anything at all.

There is no screen or kneeler inside the closet-sized room.
Just two chairs
and a small table with a book
and a candle
and a box of tissues.

I can tell the priest is tall and thin although he is seated
and wearing the long shapeless robes of his office.
He smiles at me with large white teeth
brilliant against his dark skin
and gestures for me to sit in the chair opposite him.
I am immediately relieved
that he is young and lacks the stern serious gaze
I expect from a confessor.

As soon as I'm seated, I fold my hands in my lap
as much to keep them from shaking as to appear pious.
Keeping my eyes locked on them, I begin.

"Bless me, Father, for I have sinned.
It's been two years since my last confession."

I pause here, waiting for his instruction
to confess my sins, but the priest is silent.
A surreptitious peek reveals
that his head is bowed, and his eyes are closed
as if he is as humbled as I to be sitting here.
So I continue and tell him everything.

My voice begins to quiver and the tears spill
from the corners of my eyes and over my nose
less from a penitent heart than for fear of reproval.
Finally, I look directly in his face
and say, "But I don't see why it's wrong
to be with someone you love."

Father hands me a tissue and waits for me
to blow my nose and wipe my face.

"It is never wrong to love someone," he begins
in a musical accent I don't recognize
confirming he's likely a visiting priest who I'll never meet again.
"But you described the pain your family is going through
because of your actions
and it seems that you are also in pain
due to the hurt you've caused.
Do you think it might be God's grace
that allows us to experience this regret
when we have sinned?"

And that makes perfect sense to me.

I don't regret loving Steve and being with him
but in those moments, we thought only of ourselves.

Suddenly, I do deeply regret
this grief that we caused our parents
who mourn the loss of the people they thought we were
and could have been.
It is not only Steve and I
who will suffer the effects of our actions.
It was selfish, careless, and childish.

When I begin my Act of Contrition
it is no lie to say, "Oh my God
I am sorry for my sins
with all my heart…"

I am late for school.
Again.

The earlier I get up, the sicker I am
so I try to wait until the last possible moment
but the seven-mile drive takes at least 45 minutes
in the rush-hour traffic, if there are no accidents.
At least I don't have to pick up Steve today
since Bill gave him a lift.

I still lose time, thanks to my stomach
when I have to pull over
to vomit onto the floor of the passenger seat.
I wipe my mouth with a towel I keep in the car for this purpose
and lay it on top of the puddle of bile.

Steve is looking at the door
when I walk into Mr. Adam's first period class
fifteen minutes late.

"Miss Dietsch, how nice of you to join us.
How many times is that now? Five or six?
I think that means you will have to make up the time
after school."

He hands me the first detention slip of my school career.

After class
Steve runs out to the parking lot to clean out my car.
And I head to Mr. Tolbert's office
again
to see if I can drop first period.

I just can't do this anymore.

I wake up suddenly
with the dip of the bed
when someone sits next to me.

I roll from my side on to my back, peering into the dark.

"Mom told me," my sister whispers.

I'm not awake enough to say anything yet.
I don't understand what she wants.

I look at the clock on my dresser
and notice it's 6:32 pm.
I must have fallen asleep after practice again.
I sit up, confused.

Colleen never comes into my room
except to borrow clothes
or yell at me for borrowing hers.
But she doesn't even live here anymore.

What is she doing here?

I notice she has been gripping my arm
this whole time.

"What?" I mumble, rubbing my hand over my face.
"Is it time for dinner?"

"Mom told me you're pregnant."

I don't know what to say.
One more person knows my secret.
I stare at her
waiting to see what she will say next.

Colleen and I were best friends
when we were little
but not since she was 12 and I was 10.
All of a sudden, I was stupid and annoying

and she was cranky and aloof.

Since then she's been a bit of a rebel
and considers me a member of
The Establishment
because no matter how much she tries to fit in
it's never as easy for her
as it is for me.
She was never a bad kid.
She just doesn't know how to be
who Mom and Dad seem to want her to be.
I can't understand why
she makes everything so hard
and she doesn't understand why
I'm such a pushover.

I can't say I've even missed her very much
since she moved out.

So I just look at her.

Is she here to scoff
at my stupidity or gloat
over my shame?
I won't even try to defend myself this time
because I know she's right.

She says, "I know they thought I would be the one
to get pregnant."
Then I notice her chin begins to tremble.
"Oh Kelley..." her whisper quavers.

I'm not sure if she's upset for me
or relieved for herself
not to be the only one
who is a disappointment this time.

"What are you going to do?"

I shake my head and shrug at the same time

and then she pulls me to her and hugs me
and whispers over my shoulder, "I love you."

Now I am the one who is relieved
and I hug her back.

I wonder if this means
we are on the same side again.

The school nurse is here, at my house.
She meets my mother
and takes a tour of our home.
Then she asks me about my plans
for after the baby's birth
to which I say, "I don't know yet."

I tell her about Steve, his parents, and "therapy".

She is here less than an hour, but I am still relieved
when finally, she says
"You obviously have all the support you need.
I don't see any reason to come back."

Good.

Homecoming

last year, was three weeks after Steve and I had our first date.
It was my first date ever to a school dance
and it was the night he told me he loved me too.

I can still smell the misty rain that clung to our clothes
and the wood smoke from the Halloween bonfires.
I remember how Steve smiled for pictures
with his lips pressed tightly together to hide his braces.
I borrowed Colleen's royal blue dress with just enough ruffle
to conceal that it was a little too small on top
and my mom's necklace with diamond and sapphire-colored crystals.

Steve was proud to drive us to the dance in his dad's new Camry
the windows all steamed up from our breath.
He sang along softly to a Depeche Mode song
on a new mixtape he made for the occasion
while holding my hand on the edge of the seat
stroking my thumb with his.
A song about lovers together forever.
I wondered breathlessly, had he purposely picked songs
to tell me how he felt?

It seemed like my life was on the cusp of beginning
and I could have anything, do anything
I wanted.

For this year's Homecoming, I want to pretend
that nothing has changed.
I want to be a normal seventeen-year-old worrying about
who will save us a seat at the football game
what color corsage will go best with my dress
and how far we will go in the back seat of his car.
Forget about everything else
for just one day.

We stayed late into the night at school all week
decorating the senior hallway in an outer space theme
with paper, paint, foam, and a smoke machine.
We sold paper chain links to raise money

and we created a float for the parade
where Brian and Mark's band, Spot, will play
the Homecoming theme song, *Magic Carpet Ride*
dressed as garbage bag aliens.

At the Homecoming football game, they announce
that our class has won all three contests easily.

"SWEEP! SWEEP! SWEEP!" we chant.
No one has more spirit than the class of '88!

We cheer for Brian and Steve Yates on the Homecoming court
as they ride around the track
sitting atop the back seat of flashy convertibles
and for our quarterback
when he throws touchdown after touchdown.

> *Hit 'em high*
> *Hit 'em low*
> *Hit 'em where the Trojans go!*

The day is stuffed with all the things
that make every beloved John Hughes movie.
All that's left is the romance of a special dance
with best friends and favorite tunes.

I bought a strapless T-length dress with a black velvet bodice
and a shimmery green skirt, layered over black tulle.
It has a wide sash over the stomach tied in a large bow on my hip
easily disguising my widening waist.
My long auburn hair has been permed into tight frizzy coils
that lay full and fluffy around my shoulders and down my back.

Steve holds the white rose corsage to the top of my dress
with one hand, looking for a place
to pierce the pin through the velvet fabric
without impaling me or his finger.
Leaning in further, he whispers in my ear
"You're beautiful, and you might want to do this part yourself
if you don't want blood on your dress."

In the Camry on the way to the school gym again this year
everything feels very familiar and safe.
R.E.M. is singing about "... *the one I love.*"

Steve is tapping the drumbeats on the steering wheel
with two fingers of each hand.
My forearm is resting on his shoulder
while I finger the small locks of his darkening hair—
the highlights having faded with the summer sun.
It's grown longer than usual and is beginning to curl up
just above his collar.

He turns and smiles at me
reaching across my lap for my other hand.
"This is my favorite view of you—
sitting next to me
holding my hand
and looking at me
out of the side of your cat eyes."

The gym is decorated with blue and gold streamers and balloons.
The large glaring fluorescents are turned off
and a disco ball spins colored lights on everyone
like lasered confetti.
All the Spoofers are here and dancing.
We jump giddily into the middle of the group
and lose ourselves in the music.

Stomping to Depeche's *More than a Party.*
Moshing to R.E.M.'s *It's the End of the World as We Know It.*
Spinning to The Cure's *Just Like Heaven.*
Swaying to U2's *With or Without You.*
For a couple of hours Steve and I forget about everything else.
The secrets.
The lies.
The mistakes.
The losses.
For a couple of hours, we are just seventeen.

When he touches me now
there isn't the conflict
of desire and restraint
that was palpable
when we used to make love.

I don't have to shush my conscience's warnings.
And he doesn't hold his breath
through slow, tentative movements.

We are free from the fear of unimaginable consequences.
The worst is already realized.
We discover solace and compassion
in the honesty of one another's bodies.

But it is still a furtive love
when you choose the virtue of the sin
over the lie of the penance.

NOVEMBER

Jenny's locker is right next to mine

so I usually meet her here several times a day.
I am reaching up to grab my English notebook off the top shelf
when she arrives.

"Hey, Kel. What's up?"
She opens the blue metal door and smiles at me
as she begins swapping folders and books out.

"Hi, Jen. Nothing new."

I turn to smile back at her
and notice that her eyes seem to have dropped to my waist.
A jolt of electricity rises from my stomach to my face
and I snatch my arms down
making sure my shirt hasn't pulled up
revealing my swelling skin.

"Hey, don't look at my belly!" I scold
trying to make my voice light, like I'm teasing.

"I wasn't," she denies.

She closes her locker and leans against it
holding her books against her chest.

"Are you okay?" she asks quietly.
"You've been out sick an awful lot.
I hardly ever see you anymore."

I so want to tell my best friend what I'm going through
but how can I?
I've never even told her that Steve and I are having sex.
I can't just blurt it out here, in the hallway between classes.
And then what? See ya at lunch?

"There's nothing going on. Everything is fine," I say
closing the metal door and spinning the lock.

I look away from the hurt I see in her eyes.

Of course, she knows I'm lying.

"Gotta go."

I turn and head down the hall to my next class
wondering if I've lost my friends anyway
even if they don't already know.

Calculus isn't that hard
not as hard as pre-calc was
just like his teacher Mr. Knudson had promised
but Steve prefers studying with friends
rather than alone in his bedroom.
Honestly, if it wasn't for them inviting him to join them
he probably wouldn't study at all.

They take turns meeting at each other's houses.
Today Steve and Julie are at Becky's house
sitting at the kitchen table.
Their textbooks, notes, and pencils litter the surface
along with Oreo cookie crumbs and soda cans.

"No Bundt cake, Bec?" Steve asks.
"I think we need a Bundt cake to properly prepare for this exam."

Julie laughs, recognizing one of the funny visuals
Mr. Knudson uses during his lessons
to help make the abstract become more concrete.
"Or a Jell-O mold. We could eat Jell-O too."

"Sorry, guys, it's bring-your-own-trumpet-bell
to all calculus study parties," Becky adds.
"But we've got Doritos if anyone wants some of those."

"I wouldn't say no," says Steve.

Becky hops up and rummages around in the pantry.

Julie takes this break in their studying to change the subject.
"So I guess you have been lucky
not to catch whatever Kelley has been sick with
so much this year, huh?"
The question in her voice feels like a hint.
Or a challenge.

Becky and Julie are too smart to be fooled
by his repeated explanations of "virus" or "stomach flu"
for Kelley's frequent tardiness and absences.

Even if they've guessed it, Steve can't bring himself to confirm it.
His throat tight, he takes a sip of his Sprite.
"Yeah," is all he can squeak out.

"Maybe what she's got isn't contagious, Julie," Becky suggests
as she rejoins them at the table
with a bowlful of orange dusted tortilla chips.
The cloying smell of their spice suddenly turns Steve's stomach.

"It's getting late. I have to get home for dinner."
Steve stands up and starts gathering his books and papers.

"We were just kidding, Steve," Julie quickly adds.
"We don't have to talk about it. Don't go."

Steve carelessly shoves everything into his backpack
and slings it on his shoulder as he pushes in his chair.
"No, it's not that. I just really have to go.
See you guys tomorrow."

Walking to his car, his heart hiccups rapidly in his chest.
He knows that whatever kind of test he just took
he thoroughly failed.

The craving
compels me
to pull open the refrigerator door.
My mouth practically aches
for the tart sweetness
that bites my tongue and cheeks.
A citrus explosion
flushing my throat
with cool, scarlet ambrosia.
Oh, the heaven
that is a tall glass
of chilled cranberry juice.

"Someone named Carolyn is on the phone!"
my brother yells to me from the living room.

She was my best friend in Charleston.
We met in 3rd grade at Divine Redeemer Catholic School
and were inseparable up until the day I moved
the summer after 8th grade.
Surprisingly, I wasn't devastated to say goodbye.
I looked forward to a fresh start for high school
in a new place, with new adventures.

Friendship between girls in middle school
is fraught with paradoxes.
She is your closest ally and your harshest enemy.
A single word from her
can fill you with soaring pride
or crush you with suffocating shame, sending you to cringe
behind your awkward pubescent bravado
until the return of her favor.
Her opinions matter more than anyone else's.
No parent
teacher
or older sibling
knows or understands more, what your life is like
than your best friend.

I was definitely a worker bee to Carolyn's queen.
I lived in her shadow
literally, as she was a good six inches taller than me
and socially, as I drafted in the wake of her popularity
tucking myself under the hem of her unshakable self-assurance.

I loved her.
And I envied her.

She was effortlessly smart.
Nothing less than an A on every report card.

Entrancing to preteen boys
with her grapefruit breasts

sun-browned skin
and blond Farrah Fawcett spirals.

Practically an only child, she did not share
space, belongings, or attention
with anyone.

I adored her courage and mischievous sense of humor.
She made me try things that I was too afraid to do on my own —
watching rated R movies on HBO after her parents went to bed
or feigning coughing fits in class in order to cover the sound
of her stomping walnuts on her clipboard
for a snack.

I longed for her clothes
purchased from department stores
tagged by Polo, Izod, and Guess
and all her own—
handed down from and to
no one.

I wanted her bedroom
with its full-sized canopy bed
and pink curtains fringed in white pom-poms.

Mom always told me
that I was prettier, smarter, and more athletic than Carolyn
and that she loved coming to our house
because hers was too quiet and boring
but none of that made any sense to me.
It was obvious to everyone I knew
that I had nothing
that Carolyn could ever want.

She had everything, was everything.
We could not be more different
which is why I wanted to be just like her.

But after my first year in Gaithersburg
I stopped missing Carolyn.

I made new friends
who didn't compel me to expend so much energy
trying to be them.
I hadn't spoken to her on the phone in over a year
and our letters have slowed to almost a standstill
so I am stunned to learn that she is waiting for me
to pick up the phone.

"Hello?"

                                    "Hi Kelley! It's Carolyn!"

"Hi Carolyn! What a surprise!"

                                    "Oh my God, it's been so long!
                                                How are you?"

"I'm doing great. What's up with you?"

I listen with a few "wow"s
and an occasional "that's awesome"
while Carolyn tells me all about her boyfriend
—a cadet from the Citadel—
and the drudgery of writing all those essays
for her college applications
and the never-ending demands
as the student chair of the graduation committee.

Finally, she gets around to the real goal of her call.

                        "Can you come down for Christmas break?
                        I already contacted Christina and Kathleen
                                    and they are both coming.
                                    Won't it be awesome
                        to have the whole gang back together?"

It does sound wonderful.
Hanging out with my old friends.
Showing them who I'd become since I'd left.
It would be so much fun being with Carolyn

knowing I was her equal.
Except now I'm not.

I know that there is no way that I will go.
How can I see any of them like this?

"Well, what do you think? Can you come?"

"Oh, um, that would be amazing.
But I'm not sure.
I have to ask my parents, of course."

I chew my lip, trying to figure out
how I will get out of this.

"My mom can talk to your mom
if you think that will help.
We're all going to stay at my house.
It's going to be so fun!"

I tell Carolyn I will call her back.

———

It takes several days
to come up with a reasonable lie
and ten minutes' worth of courage
to say it aloud.
Something about studying for exams
and visiting college campuses in Boston with my boyfriend
that somehow I'd forgotten about when she called last time
and I am so disappointed
that I can't come to Charleston for Christmas.

Maybe next summer.

I can feel the music
thumping through the living room floor
where we are sitting around a coffee table in Jenny's house.
Steve and Yates have commandeered the stereo in the basement
and strains of Depeche Mode and R.E.M. float up the stairwell.

Julie takes a swallow from her can of Miller Lite
and looks at me from across the table, holding my can of Coke.
"Why aren't you drinking, Kel?"

I hardly ever drink
because it makes me say and do stupid stuff
so I assumed my established role of goody-two-shoes
would prevent anyone from questioning my virtuous sobriety tonight
but Julie is too observant and straightforward
to make assumptions.

"I can't. I'm on medication," I stammer
which is true, if you count prenatal vitamins and iron tablets.

"For what? Is it why you've been absent so much?"

Jenny sits down between us with an annoyed sigh.
She takes a sip of her berry-flavored wine cooler
seemingly to gird her for the trials of the night.

I pretend I've been distracted from Julie's question.
"Hey, Jen. What's up?"

"Ryan and Dan are getting a little wild down there
and knocked over a lamp.
They broke the bulb, but the rest of it seems okay.
What's going on up here?"

While Jenny explains the latest casualty of the evening
Julie stands up, wobbling a little
as she heads to the powder room near the front door.

"Nothing really. We were just chatting about midterms."
Our eyes follow Julie's progress to the bathroom.

Jenny giggles, "I think Julie's maybe a little drunk."

"Yeah, just a little," I scoff.

When Julie returns she is holding a small gold tube in her hand.
"What do you think, guys? Is this a good color for me?"
She plucks the lid off the cylinder and twists the bottom
to reveal the chiseled tip of a deep wine-colored lipstick.
"It's called 'Ladies' Night'. Sounds perfect to me."

Julie returns to her seat on the floor
setting the lipstick cap on the table.
She holds the dark maroon shade up next to her mouth
to give the color the backdrop of her skin tone.

"Julie, I don't think you should be using Jenny's mom's lipstick.
You must be pretty drunk," I state the obvious
and the irrelevant, as far as she is concerned.

"I think it might be too dark for you, Juls," Jenny adds sincerely.
"Your skin is too pale for it."
She takes the tube out of Julie's hand and slides the cap back in place.

Julie doesn't seem bothered by any of this
and turns back to me like a dog with a bone.
"Kel, you never answered my question.
What is the medication for?
You don't seem like you're really sick right now."
And then she adds, "Maybe only in the mornings?"

Jenny puts the lipstick on the table and looks at me
waiting for an answer.
Clearly she has been wondering this too
but isn't drunk enough yet to ask for herself.

"Julie," I say quietly, "I'm not going to talk to you about this now.
You're drunk."

I think I felt it.
I lie in bed on my back.
Breath shallow.
Palms pressed to the space below my navel.
Listening with my fingertips.

There it is.

A flip of a fishtail in a pond.
A ripple of a raindrop in a puddle.
A twist of a teaspoon in a coffee cup.

There he is.

DECEMBER

———

Steve arrives carrying a pepperoni pizza
when he comes to pick me up to go to the movies.

It's one of only about ten things he eats:
Pizza
Hotdogs
Green beans (preferably right out of the freezer bag)
Potatoes (french fried or mashed)
White bread
Rice
Peanut butter
Meat (including chicken, steak, and ham)

Nothing with sauces, dips, gravies, or condiments.
The plainer, the better.

He still carries the label of "picky eater"
that most of us outgrew in middle school.
He is unashamed and unapologetic about it.
If you serve him something he doesn't like
he won't complain, but he won't eat it either.
He'll just pick up a pizza later.

I sit with him at the kitchen counter and wolf down a slice.
Then we go down to the family room
to let my parents know we are leaving
which gives me just enough time to realize
that the pizza is coming back up.
I rush to the bathroom and return in five minutes
already having brushed my teeth.

"Do you want to just stay in?" Steve asks
rubbing his hand across my back.

"No, I'm actually fine now. Let's go."

At the theater, I decline the candy and popcorn
requesting a vat of Coke instead
which I hope will settle my stomach
even though it will create an alternative discomfort

that will have to be addressed
before the end of the movie.

Yates and his date, Cathy, sit on the other side of Steve.
I'm glad because I don't really know her
and don't feel like acting interested in her life
which is what I'd have to do
to keep her from having time to ask me anything about mine.

As the lights go dim, I slouch down in my seat
and feel Steve rest the back of his hand on my thigh
palm up, fingers spread in silent request.
I answer with mine.
He uses his free hand
to pour peanut M&Ms into his mouth from the bag.
Then he holds it out to Yates, offering him a handful.
Yates peels off a rope of cherry Twizzlers in exchange
and then leans forward in his seat to offer some to me.
Steve nudges me.

I look up to Yates' outstretched hand holding the Twizzlers
and his eyes staring, locked somewhere around my lap.
I shake my head no to the candy as I follow his gaze.
I assume I've spilled something on my sweater
but as I wipe my hand over my stomach
I realize that there is a noticeable bulge in my silhouette
brightly lit by the movie screen.

Shit.

Sitting upright, I quickly pull my hand free from Steve's
and cross both my arms over my midsection.
Suddenly I urgently need to pee.
Whispering in Steve's ear, I escape to the bathroom
where I study my profile in the mirror.

Maybe he'll just think I'm getting fat.

I'm going to have to quit Asbury soon.
I've traded in my uniform a couple of times already
for larger sizes.
The fitted bust and waist of the dress
make my expanding shape difficult to hide.
The apron helps, but soon my supervisors will notice
even if the bifocaled residents won't
for at least a couple more months.

Jenny comes into the locker room as I'm changing
out of my uniform.
I turn my back to her, hoping she doesn't see anything
before I get my bulky sweater pulled over my head.
Usually this room is filled with several other chatty waitresses
at the end of the dinner shift, comparing stories about surly residents
or messed up orders from the kitchen
but today it's just Jen and me.

She plops down on the bench next to me
facing in the opposite direction
and pulls her hair net off and stuffs it into her apron pocket.
I bend over to untie my white canvas shoes
with the required rubber soles, spreading my legs a little
to make room for the small bulge of my belly.
Jenny is unmoving next to me.

"Kel, when are you going to tell me what's going on?"
she asks quietly.
"I'm so worried about you."

I freeze for a moment, curled over my lap
with my fingers tucked under my shoelaces.
Pulling my shoes off, I sit up again
staring straight ahead at my open locker
not focusing on anything in particular.

"Why won't you tell me?
I'm your best friend, Kel. I want to help."

Swapping my white shoes for the pair of black flats in my locker

I slip my feet in them while pulling on my coat.
Slinging my purse over my shoulder, I gently shut the locker door.

"I can't, Jenny," I finally whisper, "I just can't talk to you about it."

As I leave the room, I turn and look at Jenny.
Her eyes are wet, and her nose is pink
with the tears she is holding back.

"I'm sorry, Jen."

Everyone says
that we will lose our friends once they know.
The break won't be intentional or abrupt; it will happen slowly
over months
as life's road signs necessarily point us
in different directions.

Friends are the ones who love you for who you are
right this moment
unlike your family, who loves you mostly
for who you were when you were little
and who they hope you will become in the future.
Steve and I know the Spoofs love us enough
not to abandon us outright, but eventually
they will move on.

They have to.

And we will be left behind
with diapers and daycare bills.
We can't blame or condemn them, but it is obvious
that as soon as they know I am pregnant
a divide will begin to open between us and them
that will grow into an impassable chasm
the day the baby is born.

                                              Unless we give it away.
                                                            Then
                                                          maybe
                                              we can start again.

But everyone will still know.
And it will be awkward and weird.
Because we will want to forget it, yet no one really can.
So it will probably still be over.

Either way, we lose.

But I don't know how to do problems alone.

My parents are dealing with their own trauma now
mourning my lost potential.

And Steve shuts it all into a small box that he only opens a crack
when someone makes him.
I know he won't leave me
but it feels like a desperate holding on
like I'm the only thing keeping him from going under.
He has no idea what he wants.
He won't even let himself ask that.
He just keeps trying to make everyone else happy.
His parents.
My parents.
Our friends.
Me.
He keeps telling all of us what we want to hear
hoping that will fix what he broke.

For me, pretending everything is fine all the time
has become just as scary and lonely as I imagined it would be
if I told the truth.

So I think that is why
I finally give in.

Jon and I
walk out Asbury's back door together.
It's only been dark a couple of hours, but the black sky
and my spent body
makes it feel close to midnight.
My breath steams from my mouth as I sigh my exhaustion
into the frosty December air.

We divide at the bumper of my car
and I toss, "See you tomorrow" toward the dark sky
as I lower myself behind the steering wheel.
I turn the ignition and immediately crank up the heat
blowing into my cupped fists.

A tapping on the passenger window makes me jump
and I look up to see Jon's blurred image
floating behind the frosted glass.
I lean over to pop the lock, and he climbs in
and shuts the door behind him.

What is he doing?

His little blue Triumph is parked in the spot right next to mine.
I assume he wants to talk, but I don't want to.
Jon has this way of getting you to tell him your secrets.

He doesn't keep me guessing for long.
"What is it, Kel? What's going on?"

"What do you mean?" I take a deep breath
and let out a tired sigh, leaning back against the vinyl headrest
and close my eyes.
"Nothing's going on. I'm just tired."

"I feel like there's something wrong with you.
You're never around.
Even when you're here, you're not really.
Steve sticks next to you like you're going to break
and he needs to be there to pick up the pieces."

I don't respond.

I keep my eyes closed and clench my teeth
but the tears slip out anyway, gliding down my face
over the lip of my hardened jaw and slide stickily down my neck.
I catch them at my collarbone and rub them in.

It is getting harder and harder
to rebuff the constant questions from everyone.

"Are you sick? Is it serious?"

I swallow, lick my lips, and then pinch the skin
inside the right corner of my lower lip between my teeth
trying to stop the words.
But I am just so tired. So very tired.

I hear Jon breathing, but he doesn't speak.
Then I feel his hand gently rest on top of mine lying in my lap
below the small swell of my expanding middle.
"It's okay, Kel," he says.

A short, wet groan escapes my lips. "I'm not sick. Not really."

He waits silently.

Then the fear suddenly leaves me, and I can't remember anymore
why I've been carrying this lie around for so long.
I feel like it's been anchoring me underwater all this time
while I hold my breath and fight fruitlessly for the surface.
Now I finally realize it is so much easier
to stop resisting the inevitable.
Simply inhale and let the darkness in.

"I'm pregnant, Jon."

The silence feels anxious now.

Finally he says, "I didn't even know you and Steve were having sex."
He sounds genuinely shocked.

"Why is that so hard to believe, Jon?
Because we didn't tell anyone?
Because I'm too much of a goody-goody?"

"No. I don't know. I had no idea.
I'm sorry, Kel."
Then he puts his hand on my back between my shoulders
and pulls me into a hug.
"Are you okay? What are you guys going to do?" he asks softly.

"I don't know. We don't know.
Please, don't tell anyone."

I am numb.
No fear or relief.
Nothing.
It really is so much easier to just let go.

I lock myself in my room.
My heart is thudding in my chest, and my hands are shaking
as I punch the clear square buttons on the phone.

On the drive home the panic returned.
How will I explain to Steve what I have done?

Mrs. Smith answers and tells me to hold on a minute.
She yells for Steve to pick up the other line.
I chew on the inside of my cheek
trying to think of how I will tell him.

Steve picks up the phone and yells, "Got it!"
and waits for the click of the other receiver before he speaks.
"Hello?"

"Hi. It's me." I try to sound cheerful.

"Hey. How was work?" I can tell he's in a good mood.

I am about to ruin it.

"It was fine. Are you doing homework?"
I don't even know how to start to say it.
I hope he can't hear how quickly my breath is coming.

"Yeah. What are you going to do now?"

I lick my dry lips and swallow.
"Um, I have to tell you something, Steve."

"What's wrong? Are you okay?"

It doesn't sound like he's really worried.
I can hear he's playing Depeche Mode's latest album again.
The familiar chords of *Never Let Me Down Again*
pulsing behind him.

I feel like I have a ball of ice in my stomach.
I know that I've betrayed his trust.

How could I have told someone without asking him first?
He whisper-sings along as he waits for me to speak.

"I'm afraid you're going to be mad at me."

He stops singing. I can hear him breathing. Waiting.
"Why?"

"Jon knows. I told him. After work. He asked me what was wrong,
and I just couldn't lie anymore. But it's okay, I think. He was really
supportive. And he promised not to tell anyone. I trust him."

I rush to get it all out at once
hoping he will pass quickly through shock and anger
and get to understanding and forgiveness
before it's his turn to speak again.

"Steve?"

"You told him? He knows?" His voice sounds strangled
like he's about to cough.

"He said he wants to talk to you. He's going to give you a call."

His breath is pushing through the phone in quick little huffs.
"I'm sorry, Steve. I didn't plan it. It just came out. I'm so sorry."

And I realize that he's crying.
I feel panic rising up my throat. What have I done?
"Steve, it's okay. It's going to be okay."

In the background David Gahan is singing
about his best friend.

I hear a click and then the dial tone.

How could she do that?
Steve rests his forehead in his hands, his shoulders shaking
with the choked sobs he tries to stifle
so his mom won't hear on the other side of the door.

And now Jon wants to talk to him.

Steve snatches the phone receiver off the hook
shoves it in the top drawer of the desk
and slams it shut.

His breath comes so fast he feels a little dizzy.
Slipping off the chair onto the floor
he curls into a ball
trying to make himself as small as possible.

I fucked up so bad.
They're all going to hate me now.

I stand on the doorstep
afraid to ring the doorbell.
Will he refuse to see me?
I hate for his parents to see us not getting along.
They will think that they are right about us.

> *There is no way they can ever survive this.*
> *They are just infatuated teenagers who think they know what real love is*
> *but they aren't ready for real life yet.*
> *This is going to break them*
> *and the sooner it does, the better*
> *so they can get past this problem and move on.*
> *Pretend it never happened.*
> *Even if they can never really forget it.*
> *It will become like a bad dream, fading away*
> *until it doesn't matter anymore.*

Of course they think that. Who wouldn't?
It's what usually happens in this situation, right?

Mrs. Veazy's stats say
there are currently 25 pregnant teenagers at GHS.
What are the odds that any of us
will end up making happy little families?
I know what everyone thinks
because I used to think those things too, about those other girls.

> *Their parents will kick them out.*
> *They will drop out of school and go on welfare.*
> *They will live in a scary apartment or trailer park.*
> *With rotating male partners*
> *who wear Confederate flag t-shirts with the arms cut off*
> *to show their tattoos.*

But I am different.
We are different.
And I refuse to be a statistic or a stereotype.

The way I see it, we already beat the odds.
Our parents haven't kicked us out.

Steve hasn't broken up with me and run off
denying any responsibility.
We're different. What we have is special.
I know it, and Steve knows it.

I just have to make sure he remembers that tonight.

I ring the doorbell
and step back down off the small stoop
smoothing my hair behind my ears.
I notice the blinds are open on the window to the right of the door
but the room is dark.

Maxi, yipping frantically, is the first to respond.
Then the porchlight flips on.
Mrs. Smith holds the plump gray schnoodle tightly under one arm
when she pulls the door open.

"Oh, hi Kelley. I didn't know you were coming over."

"Hi. Um, I needed to get a book from Steve to do my homework.
I just spoke to him on the phone."

"Sure. I think he's just in the den there.
I don't know why he didn't answer the door.
Must have his headphones on. Go on in."

Mrs. Smith turns and takes Maxi into the kitchen
where she will treat her with a carrot.

The closed door to the den is only two steps from the front door.
I tap on it with my knuckle, but there is no response.
Slowly I turn the handle and push on the door
just enough to stick my head inside.
The room is just barely lit by the porch light
coming through the window.
I can see white papers and a couple books scattered on the desktop.

Opening the door wider, it almost hits Steve in the back.
He's lying on his side on the floor

with his knees pulled up to his chest
and his arms wrapped around his head.

I quickly slip inside and close the door.
Dropping to my knees behind him
I place my hand gently on his shoulder.
His body jerks and his eyes fly open, white and wide.
I jump back instantly, pulling my hand from him
as if I've carelessly scalded his skin with my fingers.

He glares at me fearfully, like I'm a stranger.
Then I notice he is wearing headphones and realize
he didn't hear Maxi barking or me coming into the room.
He was just startled by my touch.

Now that he sees it's me
he slides his headphones off until they are circling his neck.
Then he turns away again and lies back down on the floor
returning to the position I found him in.
I know it's not a rejection; he's choosing to hear my voice
instead of the music.

I lie down on my side next to him
fitting my thighs and knees behind his
wrapping my right arm around his waist
and resting my forehead between his shoulder blades.
His t-shirt is warm and smells of laundry detergent.
I inhale deeply, searching for the comfort of the scent of his skin.

His breath is hitched from crying and he's trembling.
"Please don't be mad at me," I plead to his back.

He sniffs loudly and wipes his arm across his face
but he still doesn't look at me.

"I'm not mad at you; I'm mad at ME.
It's all my fault. Everyone is going to hate me."

"I don't hate you," I whisper, "I love you.
We are the only thing that matters."

- 149 -

We lie there breathing together.

Finally, he rolls over and wraps his arms around my ribs
squeezing me so close no air can pass between our bodies.
He tucks his face in the crook between my neck and shoulder.
I rest my hand on the back of his head
moving my fingers in small circles through his hair.

"Shh," I croon, "it will be okay."

It's more like a push
than a pull now.
Intermittent pats and pokes
from matchstick limbs
tapping on the walls of their cozy cave.

We lie side by side
on Steve's bedroom floor next to his twin bed.
I have my shirt pulled up, scrunched under my breasts
while my hand rubs and depresses the taut skin
tracing a circular path
around the small firm protrusion of my abdomen.

My fingertips freeze on a light bump
like the nudging of a puppy's nose in the palm of my hand.

"Do you want to feel it?" I ask warily, uncertain of his response.

He props himself up on his elbow cupping his ear in his palm.
"I don't know. It might freak me out a little."

"Yeah, it's kinda weird at first.
But it's really soft and gentle, like maybe it's trying to say hello
but is a little shy."

Steve reaches out his hand
and tenderly places it on the smooth swell.
I lay my hand over his and move it to the place
just inside my left hip bone where I felt the last thump.
We both hold our breath
waiting, as if listening for a faint voice.

"There! Did you feel it?!"

Before I finish the question, Steve snatches his hand back
like he's been stung
and pushes himself up so he sits on his hip, leaning on his hand.

Startled, I grasp the hem of my shirt with both hands
and yank it down, covering my bare stomach

- 151 -

suddenly ashamed that he was frightened by my body.

But then, he slowly reaches out
and rests his hand on top of both of mine
gently guiding them up toward my chest
baring my midsection once more.

He leans closer to me, stretching his neck
as if peering into the pond of my belly
for his own reflection.

"Oh my God, that was amazing!" he whispers, staring at my midriff.

"Can I feel it again?" he asks, his eyes wide.

The five of them
stake out a couple tables
in a corner of the KFC dining room after school.
It is like always, making fun of and insulting each other
while stealing unguarded fries and bites of chicken tenders
and receiving jabs to the gut and balls in return.

It has been a while since Steve has hung out with just the guys.
He relaxes into the familiar comfort
of obnoxious banter and harmless horseplay that means nothing
and yet is the everything that is being with best friends.

As he stuffs a few more fries into his mouth
he notices that the chatter and laughter seem to slow
and then stop altogether. It is strangely quiet.
He looks up from his tray
taking a quick survey of the nearly empty restaurant
to see what caught everyone's attention.
Steve follows the group's eyes
landing on Brian sitting across from him.
They are all looking at Brian expectantly
and Brian is looking directly at him.

"What?" Steve asks
the straw of his drink poised just below his mouth.
The air in the room feels tense. "What's going on?"

It is suddenly clear
that this is not just a normal afterschool KFC hangout.
Something is about to happen.
His stomach clenching, Steve slowly lowers his cup
back onto the tabletop without taking a drink.

Brian pushes his tray aside, giving up his food
to whoever wants to snag it first.
But no one touches it.
Jim, Ryan, Yates—they are all looking elsewhere now.
Out the window.
At the girl behind the counter.

Across the red-tiled floor
covered in the litter of soiled napkins
and gristly bits of chicken bones.
They ignore the food and Steve's questions
as if they are embarrassed for him.

They know what's coming. They've planned this.
Steve's eyes flick to the door
imagining he might escape this ambush.

"That's what we've been wondering,"
Brian says at last.
"What's going on with you and Kelley?"

Shit.

Steve can feel his pulse jump
and sweat immediately bead up on his forehead.
He can't look at Brian anymore.
The accusation, the disdain, the pity.
He doesn't want to see it in his friend's eyes.

Fuck.

"Kelley's absent all the time
and you don't hang out with us anymore.
We know something's wrong."

Steve picks up the straw wrapper on his tray
and starts twisting it around his index finger.
"Everything's fine." He tries to keep his voice casual.
"Nothing's wrong. I don't know what you're talking about."
He forces his eyes up but can't make them land
anywhere higher than Brian's chin.

He knows that they know, he is lying.

"She dropped first period, Steve, and didn't pick up anything else.
How could she do that
unless there was something totally serious going on?"

Brian's voice is gentle, not accusatory, almost pleading.
But Steve doesn't know how to say it out loud.
He hasn't said the words to anyone
since he told his mom that first day.
Maybe not even in his own head.

Clutching his hands together in his lap, he inhales deeply.
Trying to push the words out past his lips
he opens his mouth, only to snap it quickly shut again
when he feels his eyes begin to sting in the corners.
The back of his throat tightens up like a fist.
Squeezing his eyes closed, he bows his head
letting the breath out in a shaky huff.
Biting his bottom lip, he tries to prevent his breath
coming faster and louder.

"Is Kelley pregnant?"

They already know. It's over.

Sighing, Steve slouches low on the bench
leaning his head back on the wall behind him.
He pushes both hands over the top of his head
scraping his scalp with his fingers
and then grabs handfuls of his hair, tugging on it from the roots
as if he could yank his fear and anger
out of the top of his head.

"Yes," he says finally
calmly dropping his hands limply into his lap.
"She's pregnant."

Now they are all looking at him again
faces blank and unreadable.

Then Brian reaches across the table
and places his hand on Steve's shoulder, "We're here for you, man.
You and Kelley.
What do you need?"

For Christmas

Mrs. Smith gives me a coat, the twin of one she bought herself.
It's a charcoal tweed with a hood lined in scarlet felt.
It's wide and spacious, reaching to my knees
and has huge pockets.
It's shaped like a cloak with sleeves and a zipper.
Lots of room for the expanding melon of my belly.
It's just what I need. I'm touched by her thoughtfulness.

Steve calls me Red Riding Hood.

I give Steve a ring, in place of the high school ring
he didn't want.
He said it was too fat and bulky
like something a mob boss would wear
heavy and uncomfortable.
And why would he want a giant, blue, glass stone
to remember his high school after he's left it?

The ring I give him has a thin band of 14 carat gold
that doesn't dwarf his slim fingers
and a small tiger's eye stone.
Its gold and caramel-colored bands that stripe the chocolate crystal
are warm and sedate, like Steve.
I read that the gem is supposed to help you understand your true self
and diminish anxiety, allowing you to make decisions
with courage and confidence.

Steve gives me a stone as well
a fiery opal set in a heart-shaped gold pendant.
Its color changes capriciously, depending on the light
from a pale pink to a deep turquoise
with bursts of neon green and magenta
like a teardrop of bioluminescence.

It seems the opposite of the sensible tiger's eye.
Volatile. Reckless even.

Just what Red Riding Hood needs to take on the wolf.

JANUARY 1988

It may be just a coincidence
that the seemingly endless mornings of retching and gagging
finally began to dissipate
at the same time that I gave in hopelessly
to the weight of our secret.
It was too slippery and heavy to grip any more.
Slowly, finger by finger, it pulled free
until everyone knew the trouble we were in.

I felt each telling was a crack
in the quickly thawing lake on which we walked.
We braced ourselves for the expected deluge
of scorn and isolation that would come
when we inevitably fell through the ice
into the frigid waters beneath.

It is only afterwards that I realize
we are the ones who created that icy barrier
thinking it was the only thing between us and disaster.
But it had been trapping us, not them—
in the dark water below—all along.

As we expected, breaking that ice drew everyone's shocked attention
but the eyes that stared at us only waited and watched in anxiety
hoping we would take a breath
and reach for their outstretched hands.
With our friends holding on to us tightly, we soon forgot altogether
what it had felt like to be without air.

Maybe it was all that desperate grasping and clinging
to the fear and dread
that I needed to purge every morning
to get through the day.

Now I am free.

I feel safe.
Held.
Cheered.
Included.

Loved.

I am ashamed
for not trusting my friends with the care of my heart
from the beginning.

And I know
that I will never have the courage
to do what I have to do next
without them.

I feel like a teacher
telling a story to my small students.
Becky, Jenny, and Julie are spread at my feet
stretched out on the shaggy white rug
on the living room floor of my home
while I sit and sway slowly
back and forth in a rocking chair.

They take turns
reaching into the bowls of potato chips and onion dip.

The questions start easy, and I answer them simply.

"When did you find out?"

"August."

"When is it due?"

"April."

"Are you guys getting married?"

"NO!"

Being a teenage mother is bad enough
without adding child-bride to my list of mistakes.

And then the questions get a little harder.

I slide off the chair and join them on the floor
taking my turn dipping into the snack bowls.

"Will you stay in school?"

"Sort of.
I'm done at GHS at the end of the semester
but I'm still graduating with you all in June."

"What about college?"

"I'm not sure yet.
My parents want me to go.
But I haven't figured out where
or how that will work."

"Will you keep it?"

"I don't know…"

We sit in my car
in a parking lot. It's the only place we can be alone.
We both stare out the windshield
even though we can't see anything
through the rain smearing the window
because neither of us really wants to have this conversation.

"Your mom called my mom," I begin abruptly.
"She said
that you said
you want to give the baby away.
Is that true?
You told me you didn't know what you wanted."

He doesn't deny it, but his chin drops
so it's true.

"Just tell me what you want.
Please," I beg him. "I have to know."
I don't want to cry now, but I can't stop the tears.
It seems like I'm always crying these days.

The rain beats soothingly on the roof of the car
like it did on that first Homecoming night
creating a secure cocoon
for the two of us.
On that night, he touched me in a way
I had never been touched before.
I was so surprised by the unexpected pleasure and intensity
that I'd cried then too
and he held me, afraid that he'd hurt me.

But now he's a stone
voiceless and motionless.

"What do **YOU** want?" I demand now
wiping my face on my sleeve.
"You can't just keep telling everyone what they want to hear.
You have to decide for yourself."

He pulls his glasses off, squeezing his eyes shut
and presses his thumb and finger against the closed lids.

"Just tell me," I whisper.
"I can't do this alone. I need your help."

"I don't know," he finally says.
"I **don't know** what I want."

I can't think of anything else to say.
We sit in a pained silence
unable to comfort one another.

"Maybe…" he suddenly continues.
"Maybe we should think about it.
Giving the baby up for adoption."

Somehow, although I wanted it
—asked for it even—
it still hits me like a slap.
He wants to give our baby away.
He's probably wanted this all along
and has just been afraid to tell me.
Of course he doesn't want to have a family now.
That would be insane!

It's happening, what they told me to expect all along.
He's going to leave me.
That's why he's been visiting colleges with his parents
that are far away from here.
From me.
I *am* that teenage mother statistic.

"Okay," I agree, "Let's find out about adoption then."

I had a dream about the baby.
I was sitting on the beach with him
and he was a toddler already, maybe 18 months old.
Somehow I just knew he was mine.

He had dark brown hair
that curled up in a wispy halo around his head
pale, pink skin
and blueberry-colored eyes
rimmed with dark, long lashes.
He wore only a diaper.

Sitting only a few feet away from me
at the very edge of the surf
the baby poked a small shovel into the wet sand.
He giggled gleefully when the last lingering edge of a dying wave
reached out and gently licked his toes.
And then he turned to look at me
to see if I was as delighted as he.

I laughed with him, enraptured
and hugged my knees up to my chest
trying to hold onto the deliciously warm swelling
I felt expanding in my chest—
an incredible birthing of joy that almost took my breath away.

Then I heard my name being called, urgently, from behind me.
I jerked around putting my hand above my eyes like a salute
searching the area around the dunes from where the voice came.

It was Steve running toward me
with one arm outstretched, pointing.
He continued to call my name, over and over
but he wasn't looking at me.
He was looking at the sea.

Whipping back around
following the direction of his finger
I realized that the child was gone!

His red plastic shovel floated on the glassy sheet of a wave
gliding back into the ocean.

I froze
and a black well of panic began to open in my stomach.
I ran into the waves following the toy
the water only reaching the tops of my ankles
before Steve caught me by the arm.

"The shovel," he gasped, out of breath.
"Grab the shovel before it's lost!"

I stared at him, uncomprehending and speechless.

Then yanking my arm loose from his grasp
I splashed farther into the surf
up to my knees, turning, looking for anyone who might help.

I screamed, "The baby! Where is the baby?!"

But the beach was empty
besides the two of us.

Steve just stood there, watching me.
Confused and a little wary, he finally spoke
"What baby are you talking about?
There's no baby."

The adoption agency
is part of Catholic Charities.
My parents suggested we start there
to ask questions and get some information.
I am surprised by how helpful my mom and dad have been
since recently they made it very clear
that they don't want me to give the baby away.

"It's our grandchild," Mom said
"who we wouldn't get to see grow up.
A part of our family we will never know."
And then she added, "But this decision
will affect the rest of your life.
Only you can decide what is best for you."

I asked Steve to tell me what he wants, and he did.
Or what he thinks maybe he wants, so I have to do this.
Maybe he's right.

We have dressed carefully for the visit.
Steve has put on a collared shirt, khaki slacks with a belt
and brown leather dress shoes.
I am wearing a shapeless floral dress with tights and flats.
We don't want to look like high school kids
even though it's obvious to everyone that we are.

Steve holds my hand as we walk up to the front entrance.
His touch is a small comfort to me
and maybe to him too.

Inside, a little woman with a wide round face
covered by giant circular glasses and a large smile
welcomes us and takes us directly into a small office.
She gestures to the two chairs in front of a desk
covered in papers and file folders
and turns to leave.
Before she gets to the door, Steve asks her
to show him where the bathroom is.

"I'll be right back," he says to me, nervously.

Shortly, a different woman enters the room.
She is a small, smiling woman too
but she is wearing a suit, which tells me she is the one
who belongs behind the desk.

She holds out a hand and introduces herself.
"I am Flora Hernandez.
You must be Kelley. It's so nice to meet you."
She reaches me before I can stand up
so I clasp her hand from my seat.
"Are you alone today?"

"No. My boyfriend Steve is with me.
He just went to the restroom."

"Great. We will wait until he returns before we begin."
Then she fills the space with small talk.
"It is so cold outside today, isn't it?
Did you have any trouble finding us?
Was the traffic bad?"

She has started to pull some papers out of a file on her desk
and selects a pen from a cupful of them.
"How about we get started with just some basic information
while we're waiting for Steve, hmm?"

What is taking so long?

"Um, I guess that would be okay."
Abruptly, my heart starts to beat a little faster in my chest
and the palms of my hands, folded together in my lap
begin to feel sticky with sweat.

Ms. Hernandez asks me my name and birthdate
and the baby's due date.
She records each of my responses on one of her papers.
Then she asks me if I've seen a doctor.
"When was your last appointment?"

For some reason, an image of Snow White comes to mind

when she is offered that shiny red apple
by a seemingly sweet and harmless old woman.

I feel my face flush as I stammer
"We just came here for information.
We haven't made any decisions yet."
My voice sounds fast and high pitched, rising in alarm.

"Of course! This is just for our records.
We want to keep track of all our meetings
with some basic information."
She smiles broadly again.

Why does she keep saying those words, "basic information"?

Then Steve is in the doorway of the office.
He looks pale, but he smiles at Ms. Hernandez
when she stands up to greet him. Steve shakes her hand.
"I'm sorry," he says and takes the seat next to mine.

"Not at all. Kelley and I were just getting acquainted," she answers
moving to softly close the door.
Turning back to us
Ms. Hernandez begins again, "She tells me
you think you might want to give your child up for adoption."

Steve nods and she continues, once again seated behind her desk.
"First, we will need to gather information
from you, the baby's parents.
Steve, what is your full name and birth date?"

He tells her that Steven is spelled with a V
and his middle name, Garrott, is O-T-T, not E-T-T.

I wipe my damp palms across my thighs
as Steve gives her the requested information.
I watch Ms. Hernandez's pen as she records this on the paper
and without looking up, she comments
"So you'll be 18 next month. An adult."

Her eyes shift from Steve to me, and back to Steve.
"Are you still in school?" she asks us.
Her smile has faded to just a hint of a grin now.
Ms. Hernandez raises her eyebrows
pen still poised above her paper.

"Yes," Steve answers.

"And where are you living just now?"

I explain that we both live with our parents in Gaithersburg.

"I see," she stops writing and looks directly at me.
All traces of a smile gone now.
"Kelley, I notice that you will not be 18 yet when the baby is born.
Do your parents know you're here today?"

"Yes, they know. They helped me set up this appointment."

She nods and is smiling again as she writes more down in our file.
The fog of dread that has been slowly building
begins to creep up the back of my throat
and I'm beginning to feel sick to my stomach.
I think, maybe, I just bit into the apple.

When I turn to look at Steve, he is watching me.
I can see his throat move as he swallows.
He looks at me with wide, pleading eyes.

"I'm sorry, Ms. Hernandez, but I suddenly don't feel very well.
I think I need to go. Thank you for meeting with us," I say quickly.
It's not a lie exactly.
I feel like I can't stay in the office for another minute.
I have to get out of here.

Steve stands up immediately and pulls open the door.
Ms. Hernandez is standing too; her mouth open in surprise.
He holds the door open for me, ushering me through
with his hand on my back.
"Thank you," he says, leaving the door open behind us.

In the car, we wait for the defroster to clear the steamy windshield.
Steve doesn't ask me anything about how I feel
or why we left the office so suddenly
before we even learned anything at all about adoption.

Finally, I ask, "Why were you in the bathroom for so long?"

"I felt sick," he answers. It wasn't a complete lie then.

"I'm sorry, but I can't do it.
I can't give our baby away to strangers," I say.
"I wanted to do what you wanted, but I think it's too late."
It is my eyes that are pleading now.

He doesn't look surprised or upset when I say this.
He looks relieved.
I would be fooling myself
if I believe it's because he has decided he couldn't do it either.
Really, it's probably because I have made the decision
and now he doesn't have to.

"Okay," he says, twining his fingers in mine, "I love you."

His hands
are one of the things about him
that I find most beautiful.

When he slips one of his under mine
our fingers thread together automatically
and I pull the clasp of them onto my lap.

With the finger of my other hand
I trace the hills of his knuckles
pausing to rub the rough patch
at the base of his pinky
that he says is a birthmark.

His hands are small for a man's
just the tips of his fingers reach past mine
when we press our palms together.
A ring
only size 7 ½
slides easily over the narrow joints.

His fingers are straight and thin
with perfect, white half-moons
rising on each nail bed.
The cuticles are smoothly invisible.

His hands are graceful
without being delicate.
Like a musician's.

He straightens his fingers
and glides them up and down between mine
combing my skin
with his.

In this way, he says things to me
when he doesn't have the words.
Today, he is making a promise.

I'm applying to college
like the four-year kind, not just a community college
and so is Steve.
Our parents still want us to go away to school
like we always planned.
They want us to be full-time students and live on campus
like normal freshmen.

I assumed I would just have to live at home
taking night classes at the local junior college
and working during the day.
But my mom says that college teaches you a lot more
than what you learn in your classes
and it's important that I have that experience.
I should apply to colleges, and when I know where I'll be going
then we will figure it out.

How? I wonder. *How can we do that if we have a baby?*

I visited several college campuses
on school field trips my junior year.
I fell in love with James Madison University.
I imagined I could really see myself on the red brick pathways
and in the halls of the columned buildings.

But that dream really doesn't make any sense now.
I know I have to stay pretty close to home.
I decide to apply only to Towson State University
another campus I visited last year.
It's only one hour north of Gaithersburg
and I know I can get in
and that they have a good teacher's college.
I've always thought I would like to be a teacher.

Steve's parents took him to visit some out-of-state schools
and he is working on applications for several of them.
But he hasn't applied to Towson yet, and it bothers me.
Doesn't he want to go to the same school as me?

One night, after a dinner of tacos at my house

Steve and I sit close together on the couch
watching an episode of *Star Trek.*
"Did you finish your college applications?" I ask.

"Almost," he answers.

"I don't understand why you're applying to all those colleges
so far away."

"Delaware is less than two hours from here.
That's not far."

I let go of Steve's hand
and cross my arms over my chest.
We are both still looking at the tv.
even though we clearly aren't listening to it anymore.

"Well it seems far to me.
Penn State is even further. And Indiana is like *ten* hours!
Why are you even applying there?"

"Because that's where my parents went
and they want me to.
I'm just doing whatever they want.
It doesn't mean I'll go to any of them.
I probably won't even get in."

Steve is trying to reason with me.
He's not angry, but I can tell he's getting stressed
because he's twisting the short hairs of his right eyebrow
like he does when he's thinking.

I don't see how this makes sense to him.
Why would he pretend
he is going to go to school where his parents want
and then just drop a bomb
when it's time to send the money in?
Like his parents will be just fine with the sudden change in plans
after he's lied to them for six months?

But then it occurs to me—
maybe he hasn't been lying to his parents.

I'm angry now, and I'm going to make him admit
that it's *me* he's been lying to all this time.

I turn and face him now, pulling the pillow from behind my back
and holding it in front of my stomach.
I demand to know
"Why can't you tell them you don't want to go there?
Why do you have to do whatever they want you to?
Are you afraid to tell them you want to be with me?
Or is it that you really don't know
if you want that yourself?"

Now he's getting angry too
and he starts pushing a hand back and forth through his hair
making it stand up on end.
Suddenly he slaps his hands hard on his thighs
and stands up.
He's glaring down at me when he answers.

"What are you talking about?
I'm here, aren't I?
Do you think that I've been faking all this time?
That I'm lying when I say that I love you
and I want to be with you?"

I stand up too, bringing my face close to his
"Aren't you?!
If you *really* want to be with me, Steve
then why haven't you applied to Towson yet?
You don't actually plan to at all.
Do you?"

I can tell at once that I've pushed him too far.

Steve's face is red, and he is trembling with the effort
of keeping his voice from being heard upstairs
as he practically spits the words at me.

"Because maybe what I want
isn't the only thing that matters, Kelley!

Maybe I think that listening to my parents
for once
is the least they deserve
after I fucked everything up!

Or maybe
I'm just a fucking coward."

He turns and bounds up the stairs to the foyer
taking three steps at a time.

And then I hear the front door slam.

All we seem to do now
when we are together
is fight or cry.

> Often both.

I keep insisting that we should talk
about the baby
college
our relationship.

> Our future.

But Steve doesn't want to talk at all
about any of these things.

> Or he can't.

When I have a problem, I just want to tackle it.
Make a decision and act on it.
I'm passionate and decisive.

> Which can be a bad combination.

But the current situation has a hard deadline
so curbing these qualities
seems pointless and counterproductive.

I have lost my vision of who I am
and where I'm going
and I want to know what the new one is.

> Now.

But Steve doesn't think that way.
He needs to let the question marinate
soaking up the thoughts and feelings of everyone involved
until the solution simply....

> reveals itself.

I'm too impatient for that; I need a plan.

> Today.

Then once I'm on the road
if I run into a fork or a roadblock that I didn't anticipate

I just make a new plan

and quickly take a detour.

My constant demands for Steve
to move along or catch up
are just muddying his process.

So I've decided to stop insisting
that he make decisions
and take the reins myself.

I can lead the way

so long as I can trust

that he won't let go

of my hand on the path.

Please, hold tight.

I'm going on a retreat
with my church's youth group.

I don't know what to expect exactly.
I haven't been on one since my 8th grade confirmation.
It was three days and two nights of intense self-reflection and prayer.
We were awakened with overhead lights at 6:30 a.m.
and not back in our cots before midnight.

Every minute of the weekend was scheduled
with motivational speaking
journaling
discussion circles
scripture reading
and singing
interspersed with a bunch of silly ice-breaking games.
It was all-consuming, and overwhelming, and exhausting.

Just exactly the way I've been feeling at home for the past 5 months.

> If it's just going to be a lot more of the same
> what exactly will I be retreating from?

> I'm also a little nervous
> that I have set myself up to play the part
> of the biblical fallen woman
> in need of redemption.
> Now that my situation is obvious to everyone
> my role as the "good girl" seems absurd.
> Except that's how I still think of myself.
> I don't know how to play this part of a jaded teen mother.

> Yet there is something that is drawing me to a space
> where I can expect to be loved and accepted
> and, yes, maybe forgiven too.

Deacon Gene Cummins is leading the retreat.
He looks a lot like a Santa Claus in training
with his large round stomach
and a persistent twinkle in his bright eyes.

When we meet, he takes both my hands in his
and smiles broadly, making deep crinkles in the corners of his eyes
and I believe him when he says, "I'm so happy you're here, Kelley."
His son Tom is there too.
I recognize him from school, a year or two below me.
He's in training to be a firefighter and EMT.
He seems fascinated with my condition
and finds a seat close to me each time the whole group assembles.

I struggle with the nonstop schedule
feeling nauseous and prone to tears
due to the long stretches between meals and the late hours.
The sympathetic leaders
hand me packets of cheese crackers and apple juice
and let me skip out on a couple of events after lunch
to take a nap in one of their private rooms.

Despite not feeling up to everything, by the end of the weekend
I have shared and prayed
laughed and cried
hugged and hoped
and found some peace.

And Tom Cummins, weirdly, offered to deliver my baby.

Second semester of my senior year
I enroll in two classes at Montgomery College.
Instead of going to the high school every day
I'll go to MC on Monday, Wednesday, and Friday mornings
taking Introduction to Psychology and Russian History.

Other than the lack of locker-lined hallways
and the addition of ashtrays in the student cafe
I am surprised how much it feels like GHS.
Everyone still rushes into class at the last minute
toting backpacks or purses
and looking for their friend or group to sit with
preferably in the back.
I suppose most of the students are older than me, but not by much.
Except for one woman who looks about my mom's age
and sits in the front row, writing in her notebook
even before class begins
and a guy who is probably in his late twenties.
(No high school kid has that much facial hair.)

I like my teachers. (Am I supposed to call them professors?)
And the material is really very interesting.
I take lots of notes but say little.
I don't stay and chat with anyone
and head straight back to my car after the second class
to go directly to my new job.

I work at Gaithersburg City Hall now.
Brian's mom is on the City Council, and she got me a job there
doing data entry on building permits that go back 100 years.

I quit Asbury after I grew out of my uniform
for the third time.
My managers probably already guessed
but I just couldn't stay there any longer
as it became obvious to the residents.
I didn't want to see the disapproval on their pinched faces.
They used to tell me that "Kelley" wasn't an appropriate girl's name.
I can't imagine how an "unwed mother"
would affect their sense of propriety.

I am happy with my new job where I am paid more
and treated like a fellow office employee, not a charity case
to be scorned
tolerated
or just pitied.

As I approach my car in the MC parking lot
fumbling for the right key
I'm startled by someone saying hello from close by.
Looking up, I discover it's Shannon.
We were really close in 9th and 10th grades.
It was at her 15th birthday party that I first met Steve.
But Shannon and I have made new friends
and hang out with different groups now.
There was no fight or falling out.
We just gradually spent less and less time together.
By the end of last year, we hardly even ran into each other.

"Wow, I haven't seen you in a long time," she says, smiling.

I'm immediately aware of my belly bulging slightly
under my new coat.
"Hi, Shannon! What a surprise!
I didn't know you went to MC," I say
turning to face her so she can't see my profile
and holding my keys in the cradle of my hands
in front of my body.

"Yeah, I'm doing concurrent enrollment.
I have classes here in the afternoons.
I only go to the high school in the mornings.
Is that what you're doing too?"
She stands by the side of my car, shifting her books
to her other arm.
I think she may have glanced at my midsection
so she must know already.
Everyone in the whole school should know
by now.

"Yeah, but I only take morning classes."

I don't mention
that I don't go to the high school at all anymore.

"It's so much better here. High school is so pointless," she laughs.

I nod in agreement and laugh with her
although I would give anything to be there
instead of here
hiding out until my senior year is over.
Passing notes during boring classes.
Squeezing close to the Spoofers
on the benches of the crowded cafeteria tables.
Holding hands with Steve in between classes.
Running laps with Jenny at softball practice.

In college I feel like I have skipped my real life.

I am acting at being a grown up.
It's a lie.
But if I keep pretending, maybe others will believe it.

"Yeah," I say, smiling at Shannon.
"This is so much better than high school."

Just my dad and I
are heading downtown to Washington, D.C. on the Metro
to take part in the March for Life.
I have never been before
and don't really know much about the political movement
but my dad, who is a quietly devout Catholic
has six children of his own
and believes wholeheartedly that all babies are blessings
asked me to march with him
and I said that I would.

I had never spent much time
thinking about the pro-life/pro-choice debate
and hold no strong convictions about it
but I do recognize that some may see my march as hypocritical
because I had been given a choice.

I am not trying to make a statement
to other women or to the government
while I walk alongside my dad in the gray frigid weather
up Constitution Avenue.
We carry no signs and shout no slogans, but we are here
and we walk side by side with the crowd
toward the Supreme Court steps.

I suppose I do this as a promise.

To my dad
that I will take responsibility for my actions
and make up for the pain and disappointment I have caused.

And to my baby
that I will do my very best to see her safely into this world
and into a family who will love and care for her
no matter what.

At the very least, I know this.

The corner of the couch
with the best viewing angle of the tv
is Dad's favorite seat for relaxing in the evenings.
It is understood that when he comes into the room
to watch the evening news or the next episode of *60 Minutes*
the current squatter is immediately evicted.

Machen, our mixed-breed hound dog
is always the first to hear his tread
descending the stairs to the family room.
She lifts her head from its resting place on my lap
and pops to the floor like she's been stung by a bee
head ducked low, brown eyes wary as she guiltily
slinks behind the couch.

My father heads directly to the fireplace.
Opening the heavy iron door
he tosses in another log
and adjusts the glowing and crackling wood
with the black poker
before latching it closed again.
Then he walks to the couch
and drops into his cushioned spot with a sigh
while simultaneously snatching the remote from the coffee table.
Silently, he flips the channels.

When he stops, I immediately recognize the distinct piano notes
of the *Cheers* theme song.
It's impossible not to lip sync along with the words.

Dad sits with his legs outstretched and crossed at the ankles
never even glancing my way.
He is as laser-focused
and oblivious
in his quest for leisure
as with any of his workplace or household duties.

I don't care. I wasn't really watching anything anyway.
I tuck my bare toes up under the hem
of my long flannel nightgown.

Mom comes out from the tiny closet of a laundry room
carrying a basket of warm white clothes fresh from the dryer
and dumps them on the loveseat next to me.
"Help me match the socks," she says.

I pull out a collection of the long cotton tubes
and lay them flat across the top of the couch
like so many pale fish displayed at the market.
Turning up the still dingy sock soles
I look for the initial inscribed with a black Sharpie
and begin to sort them into piles.

R for Ryan   M for Michael   D for Dad

I don't need to check the A for Andrew
since his are so much smaller than the rest.

                                        Dad chuckles at something Cliff says.

Mom looks over her shoulder
squinting at the tv screen
to catch Norm's witty retort.
But I watch my father's face
which is opening into a joyful grin.

                                                  Dad guffaws loudly.

He always seems to think the dumb ones are the funniest.
I remember how he used to throw his head back
laughing out loud at *Dukes of Hazzard*'s Sheriff Rosco P. Coltrane.
I had no idea what was so funny about a bumbling policeman
but I was enamored at the sight of my usually stern father
transformed by a deep laugh and radiant smile.
I would giggle uncontrollably watching him
delighted by the magical metamorphosis.

Mom nudges me, and then jerks her head toward Dad.
She knows I want to ask him something
and is telling me this is the time.
He's happy. Relaxed. In a good mood.

I don't think he's angry at me anymore.
Not actively, anyway.
That burned out months ago.
I am treated mostly like all the others now
spoken to when there is something that needs to be said
but no small talk or casual conversation.
Dad is as frugal with words
as he is with money.
Only spent when absolutely necessary.

"Dad?"
A request for his attention during the next commercial break.

He doesn't respond.
He just stares at the tv
engrossed in the advertisement.
He's not ignoring me.
He doesn't hear me.
Laser-focused.

"Dad," I try again. Louder.

Nothing.
He's picked up the tv guide now.

"Fred."
My mother tries now.

"What?"
He looks at her, startled from his reverie.

"Kelley is talking to you," she says
and turns her back to him again
smoothing a tea towel against her thigh.

"What?" he says again
looking at me now.

"Um, I want to ask you something," I say
and smile sweetly, tilting my head

and squeezing my shoulders up toward my ears
trying to look innocent.

> Dad chuckles
> recognizing my game.
> "What do you want?" he asks
> rolling his eyes
> affecting immeasurable patience.

"Only to go on a day trip to Williamsburg
with friends, Becky and Mark.
And Steve."
My grin shows my teeth
reaching my wide eyes and raised brows
in hopeful request.

> "Oh, yeah?" is all he answers.
> "When?"

"Saturday.
Mark says he will drive."
I'm all practical now.
"We will leave really early
and be home before midnight."

> "Hmm."
> He is more serious now
> but the corners of his smile still linger.

I can see he is on the brink of agreeing.
I hop off the couch and slip to the floor at his feet.
I'm aware of how I look
in the long white flannel nightgown with small pink rosebuds.
The rounded collar and tailored cuffs button snuggly—
modestly—
at the neck and wrist.

It's the younger me.
The more innocent me.
The me of before.

I look up at him with wide pleading eyes.
"Please, Dad," I beg in a syrupy sweet voice
that we both know is part of the game.

Dad has thrown his head back now
and is laughing at the ceiling.

Then I climb up onto his lap and lay my head
on his shoulder.
"You know I'm your favorite."

My mom snorts in surprise
as I lay it on thicker
wrapping my arms around Dad's neck.

"You know it's true," I continue to tease.

Dad's face is actually flushed now.
He wraps his arm around my back
and pats my hip lightly.

"Okay, okay," he sighs
smiling at me.

"Thank you," I chirp
and give him a kiss on the cheek.
I sit there for several more minutes
while he runs his hand softly up and down my back
and smiles at Sam fighting with Woody.

I am forgiven.

FEBRUARY

The Love Bowl

is the name we gave the basketball game
because it falls on St. Valentine's Day
and is being played between a team of Spoofers
that Steve pulled together
and a team of fellow GHS classmates
who, for some reason, take rec league basketball very seriously.
It is the perfect excuse
to create a day of ridiculous fun which I have been missing out on
for weeks now, being away from school.

Taking our role of sixth man very seriously
the Spoofettes have spent the day
cutting out giant lips from red felt
and tracing on them in silver glitter glue
the self-selected nickname and number of each player
which we then attach to the boys' jerseys with safety pins.

Steve is "Fresh"
Jon is "Cassanova"
Bill is "God"
Eric is "Twin"
Matt is "Tower"
Jim is "Hurby Luv Bug"
and Dave is "Moist". (Eww, why?!)

I don't know if they mean to be ironic or enigmatic.
I suspect they are vulgar inside jokes
but Steve claims they are just being silly.

Brian arrives in a plaid sport coat and a blue tie
clutching a clipboard and pen to act as the coach for the game
which mostly means calling out meaningless plays
scoffing every time the refs make a call not in our favor
and throwing his clipboard down angrily on the gym floor.

Mark is pacing the court sideline in a long brown bathrobe
while tapping a tambourine like a hippy monk
which is the perfect soundtrack for today's absurdity.

The Spoofers play to have fun and don't care about winning.
They shoot for style rather than points.
They would hate to mess up their perfect losing record
and make sure not to try too hard.

Still, there is a casualty when Jon races for a loose ball
and is flattened by Scott, a sub playing for their own team
resulting in an ominous crack.
A couple of the guys help Jon hop to the sideline
having lost his place on the court but not his sense of humor.
He decides Scott will be called "The Bonecrusher" from now on.

It isn't until the final buzzer sounds
and another official loss is recorded
that Jon agrees to go to the ER for an X-ray
earning the team's MVP of the game.

On the road back to Gaithersburg
we might be accused of poor sportsmanship
for running a 25 mph rolling roadblock
for a few miles along the two-lane street
while the winning GHS team honks loudly behind us
riding closely on our bumpers.
But it seems hilariously well-deserved to us
as punishment for taking the game too seriously.

When they are finally able to screech past us
we wave and smile at the irate winners
feeling ironically victorious.

Steve's 18th birthday

is three days after Valentine's Day
so a surprise party planned for later that night
seems the perfect way to celebrate.
Mom and Dad helped me plan and set up for the party
allowing my friends and I to take over one whole level of the house.
I think they are just as anxious as I am
for me to feel and act like a normal teenager again.

Brian and Mark's band, Spot, is set up in our dining room.
The furniture is pushed aside to make a dance floor.
The kitchen counters are filled
with pizza, chips, soda, and a chocolate birthday cake.
Jenny and Julie have hung balloons and streamers
and a handmade "Happy Birthday" sign.

I put on a long, knit, navy blue skirt
with a roomy tan and navy sweater.
Becky helps me crimp my hair.

Everyone is here to celebrate with us.
All the Spoofers
and many more friends
and friends of friends
who don't even give my enlarged midriff a second glance.
Even Jon is here, leaning on crutches with a fresh white plaster cast
running from the hip to the ankle of his left leg
the sole—and unwanted—badge of honor
from the afternoon battle on the court.

Steve arrives
wearing a red sweater and carrying flowers for a Valentine's dinner.
He's shocked by the shouted "Happy Birthday" wishes
and I am too, a little bit
because it feels so much like before all this happened.
Everyone is genuinely happy to be here—
a party at my house, to celebrate Steve.

He smiles in embarrassed delight standing in the foyer
as friends approach him with hugs and handshakes.

Eventually, I pull him into the center of the party
pushing him down into a large wingback chair
where he can see and be seen.
I sit on his knee and lean back against his chest
his chin resting on my head
with my large belly on display.

We watch friends all around us
dance
talk
and laugh
like they always do when we're together
like nothing has changed.
I guess some things really haven't.

I stand on a kitchen chair
while Mom pins the straps
for the denim overalls she is making for me.
I have no interest in shopping
in the maternity section of JC Penney's.
The clothes there look like tents
with collars the size and shape of hang gliders.
No, thank you.

Mostly I wear baggy sweaters and stretchy leggings
which is pretty much what all the girls are wearing
at school now anyway.
But my belly has outgrown most of these
so Mom dusted off the old sewing machine to make a few outfits
to get me through the final two months.

The overalls are a pale blue twill
with a short bib that runs across the top of my breasts.
Large pleats gather below the chest and extend down to the legs
leaving a puckered balloon for the baby to fill as it grows.
I'm ecstatic with how unfettered I feel
not having an elastic band squeezing
the top of my bulging middle all day.

My body looks and feels foreign to me
like when you borrow a dress from a friend
for an unexpected one-time event.
It never fits quite right
and you spend the night tugging and adjusting it
to cover exposed skin or relieve strangled anatomy.

My distended belly is firm like the rind of a watermelon
but still malleable by the alien limbs that push from the inside
stretching and rolling my taut skin like it's made from latex.
It's becoming difficult to tie my shoes or shave my legs.
My belly button has popped out.
It pokes disgustingly like a nose through my shirt.

A faint brown line has appeared on my skin
dissecting me vertically from breastbone to pubic hair

and my nipples have gone from small shell-pink cherries
to large dark rose-colored discs.
My breasts have swelled
from a small B cup to spilling out of a C
which I expected to be an improvement, except now
they rest on the top of my belly, so my midsection
resembles the large face of a pale, bulge-eyed frog.

Both my breasts and hips are marked
by pale pink stretch marks along the sides
and I am peppered with bruises
on my hips, thighs, and protruding middle
from constantly misjudging the distance
between my body and hard objects.

My mom always talks about how much she loved being pregnant.
She was one of those women who are described as "glowing".
I just feel fat and awkward, a helpless captive
to the growing parasite within.

Mom is kneeling down and beginning to pin the hem of a pant leg
when my youngest brother Andrew walks in the kitchen
and slumps against the table, looking at us.

"Mom, when's dinner? I'm hungry."
He is seven years old, and the sixth and final child
(Please, God!)
of the Dietsch family, which means
he is pretty much left to fend for himself.
Sometime around kid number four, my parents learned
that children are a lot more resilient and resourceful
than we usually give them credit for.

Mom mumbles, "The usual time"
trying to hold onto a line of straight pins pressed between her lips.

Andrew sighs dramatically
and lays his head and torso across the table
as if in a faint from hunger.

"Can I have a snack?"

He has red in his hair, like most of us do
but his is much lighter with a lot more blond than anyone else's.
Sweaty curls cling to his neck and forehead.

"You can have a piece of fruit," is the answer.

With another deeply mournful sigh, Andrew lifts his head.
"Fine, but fruit doesn't fill me up much."

Turning toward the countertop he suddenly stops
and stares right at my large, round middle
which is just about level with his face since I'm standing on a chair.

"Do you have a basketball in there?" he asks
with a perplexed squint to his eyes.

I slap my hand to my mouth trying to stifle my gasping giggle.
Mom stands up and moves behind the chair to my other leg.

"No, Andrew," she says, kneeling down on the floor again.
"That's a baby growing inside Kelley.
We are going to have a new baby in the family soon."

"We are?" He seems both confused and delighted.
"Will it be a boy?"

"We won't know until it gets here."

"Cool. I won't be the youngest anymore!" Andrew chirps
as he grabs an apple from the fruit bowl on the counter and then
skips out of the room.

I watch my mom pull a pin from her mouth
and pause with it pinched between her thumb and index finger.
She looks up at me and our eyes meet for a beat
and then we laugh together.

"Well, that was easy!" Mom says, sliding the next pin in place.

I am due in six weeks.
Mom has pulled out an old box of baby things
still left over after Andrew.
There are a few faded crib blankets
and long-sleeved white t-shirts with flaps
that wrap across the baby's stomach and snap under each arm.

Gramma and Mom are both crocheters
so there are a couple of afghans in teals and yellows
and a matching set of cream-colored sweater, hat, and booties.

But the crib is still in the attic
and there are no diapers
or a car seat
or sheets
or socks
or pajamas.

Won't I need burp cloths
and wipes
and lotion
and powder
and baby shampoo
and that rubber bulb that sucks out their boogers?

"Should we go shopping soon?" I ask Mom
one Saturday while I help her get dinner on the table.

"Oh, there's plenty of time," she answers.
"All of you kids were two weeks late."

In the middle of the night
my bladder wakes me.
Again.
I ignore it
but it insists.

Huffing irritably, I leave my warm bed
and walk across the cold bathroom tile.
I leave the light off
hoping I'll be able to fall back to sleep quickly
until the next time I have to go.

Traitor.

MARCH

———

Lamaze Class
is held in the library of Damascus High School.
There are about ten couples
seated in a circle of chairs.

I am embarrassed
that Steve and I are obviously so much younger than anyone else
but the nurse, Linda, who leads the class is kind and welcoming.
She doesn't treat us like the kids we are.
I suppose she knows better than we do
that it's too late to spare us anything.

We watch a video of several births.
It's sweatier and bloodier than I imagined
and the baby's dark wet head
looks like it couldn't possibly fit
through the taut pink opening
without it ripping like a stretched seam
which, the nurse informs us, actually does happen sometimes.

I feel a little nauseous and guess
from the way Steve is pulling on the hairs of his eyebrow
that he isn't enjoying this much either.

After the video, Linda answers questions about pain medicines
and shows the men how to give the mothers back massages
because sometimes it hurts there the most
which doesn't make any sense to me.

At the end, just as we are leaving
she displays a collection of large lollipops
that she says are good to suck on during labor
when ice chips are the only other option.
The bright variety of colors
makes them look like a tiny balloon bouquet
clutched in the nurse's hand.
Steve buys three.

In the car, headed home, Steve says
"I don't think I can be in the delivery room."

I know exactly how he feels.

"Well if I have to be there, then so do you," I say.

"Surprise!"

I jump
when Mom and I walk in the front door of our house
from the chorus of excited voices.

I freeze there in the foyer of our home
trying to figure out what's going on.
Colleen approaches me and hands me a card
with a pastel blue teddy bear holding a pink umbrella on the front.
It says "BABY SHOWER" in bright blue lettering.

Behind Colleen, I can see the room is filled
with pink and blue balloons.
And all my girlfriends are here:
Julie
Becky
Jenny
Susan
Robin
even Wanda and Kathy from Asbury.

My little sister and brothers are hanging out
in the back of the room too.

Everyone is dressed in skirts and pastel-colored tops
and I'm suddenly embarrassed by my baggy gray leggings
and not-quite-big-enough white sweater
stretched tightly over my midriff.

Colleen stands next to me looking at me expectantly.
She's dressed up, like she came from work
in a silky white blouse and black slacks and pumps.
But it's Saturday.

I open the card she has handed me
and realize that it is the invitation she has sent out
for this baby shower—for me and my baby.

My chin begins to tremble, and my hands shake
as the tears fill my eyes, blurring Colleen's loopy handwriting.

I look at her and can't say anything
knowing the tears will escape if I do.
She pulls me in, hugging me close and whispers in my ear
"Every mother deserves a baby shower."

I turn around and reach out to hug my mom
who is smiling in satisfaction at the success of the surprise.

"This is why you didn't want me to go baby shopping!" I say.

Georgetown
is a bohemian neighborhood in Washington, D.C.
where the avant-garde meets the sordid.
It's the happening place
for the rowdy
quirky
and occasionally depraved.
Even if you aren't old enough for the teeming bars or clubs
there is a vitality that can be leached
by clinging hopefully to the edges
of the Saturday night crowd.

The Spoofer guys think it's the perfect place
to take Steve for a night of…
celebrating?
forgetting?
something like a cross between
a bachelor party and a baby shower?
or a kind of wake for his freedom
before real life hits him?

I call him early the next morning
demanding he relate every event
and nonevent
in detail.

He does, hoarsely
and with frequent deep chuckles.
I interrupt often
peppering him with questions.

I am jealous
of the time they've spent laughing together.

"Who drove?"

"Bill."

"No one else? How did you all fit?"

I can see
all seven guys
piled into Bill's small Honda
for the drive downtown.
Their long, bony limbs
and shoes the size of canoes
overlapping and tangled
like dirty laundry in a hamper.
Steve and Ryan huddled in the front passenger seat
three more squeezed across the back seat
and Jon hunched over in the hatchback space.
They passed around Jim's homemade "silly sauce"
in plastic cups poured from an aluminum flask.

I have smelled the pungent reek
of teenage boys in a tight space.
The air filled with
alcoholic belches
sweaty, capped hair
and moist, funky skin.

"Did you drink?"

"Some."

"Where did you go?"

Downtown, they floated with the current
up and down M Street
past the blue brick Commander Salamander
and the thumping music leaking from Poseurs dance club.
They stopped in Smash! Records.
He would never just walk past a record store.

"Did you buy anything?"

"No, but I wanted to."

Mark bought a green plastic derby hat
from a clearance bin for a dollar.

                              He tipped his hat at everyone they passed
                                  saying, "Top o' the mornin' to you!"

"Was he drunk?"

"I don't know. Maybe."

Then he tells me about a place in Georgetown
I've never seen.

"It's called Pleasure Chest. Jim wanted to go in."

"What kind of store is that?"

I think I can hear his mouth
stretching wide over his teeth
in a mischievous grin.

                              He tells me about the display window
                              containing a purple-haired mannequin
                                  in a red leather, studded bustier
                                      and matching G-string.
                              Another mannequin is just a black torso
                         with paper-cutout hearts taped to her nipples
                              to match the shapes printed on her panties.

"Did you go in?"

"Yeah."

"What was inside?"

                                  The shelves and racks were packed
                                  with an unimaginable collection
                               of sex games, tools, toys, and erotica.
                              Brian picked up a two-foot-long dildo
                                  equipped with electric controls
                              that made it spin, twist, and vibrate.

"What's a dildo?"

"Like a fake penis."

"What the hell for?!"

"What do you think it's for?"

Jim found a hop-along penis
the size of a ping-pong ball.
He wound it up and let it loose
to bounce frantically across the shelf
and onto the floor.

"And what is that for?!"

"Just to be funny."

The hysterical laughter
brought the store clerk out from behind the counter.
He bent down and carefully picked up the pulsing toy.

Placing it in his cupped hand he said
"Guys, you have to be gentle with him.
Treat him like the real thing."

Then he lightly stroked
the side of the tiny plastic phallus
with a single tender finger.

"Oh my God! What did you do?"

"Jim bought it."

"Of course he did."

Eventually, they were kicked out
when Brian snuck up behind Bill
and placed the giant humming sex toy
between his thighs.

"Did he get in trouble?"

"No, he just told us not to come back."

On the way home
they had to pull over.

"Why? Did someone puke?"

"No, we had to piss."

Bill pulled over at one of the many overlooks
off the George Washington Parkway
which all claim to be "scenic".
The guys lined up on a low stone wall
and peed into the dense trees and brush
far above the Potomac River.

A swath of bright lights tracked across their backs
as another car pulled into the overlook.

"You were all caught
literally
with your pants down?"

"Yeah.
And by a cop."

"Shit!"

The police officer parked his cruiser along the curb
and turned on a bright spotlight
illuminating the group as they hastily zipped up
and jumped down from the wall.

"Oh my God, what did he do?"

"Before he could say anything, Bill ran up to him."

He waved his empty hands at the cop, and declared
"No booze, officer! No booze!"
which was true

since they had just pissed out the last of it.

"What did the cop say?"

"He let us go."

Because the police officer knew
what they had been trying to disguise all night.

They are not the men they pretend to be.
Hope to be.

The man I need him to be.

They are still
just a bunch of stupid, harmless boys.

I don't feel right—
tired, achy back, a little nauseous.

The Lamaze nurse kneels down in front of me
and places her hands along the sides of the large mound
holding still like she's listening with her fingertips.

"Braxton Hicks," she declares. "False labor."

A tightening spreads across the breadth of my taut abdomen
clenching forcefully for a couple breaths until releasing.
It feels like my belly has become a large fist.

squeeeeeeeeeze

relax

squeeeeeeeeeze

relax

I rub the firm flesh in a circular motion
like a Buddha.

Steve's eyes flit to the rearview mirror
every couple of minutes, checking on me
reclined in the back seat of my car
as he drives me home.

"I'm not leaving you tonight," he says
when our eyes meet in the mirror.

"The nurse said it's just false labor," I answer.
"And I'm not even due for two weeks."

"I'm staying."
And his tone tells me not to bother arguing.

Steve lays next to me
on my bed. The room is dark, but I know he's not sleeping.
He's lying on his side on top of the covers facing me
holding my mom's watch.

The contractions haven't stopped
like the nurse said they would.

Before she went to bed, my mom came into my room
and knelt down next to Steve, handing him her watch.
She whispered that he should start timing my contractions —
how long they last and how much time in between.

That was a couple of hours ago.

Now they are five to seven minutes apart
about 60 to 75 seconds long.
It doesn't hurt too much.
It's a lot like intense menstrual cramps.

We doze off in between.
I tap Steve with my hand to let him know when it starts
and again when it stops.
He whispers the numbers after each one
and we doze off again for a few minutes.

A lot of the laboring seems to be simply waiting.

I sit up with a gasp
as an explosion of warm liquid gushes from between my thighs.
My clothes and the sheets are sopping.
Steve is sitting up too.

"Did I just actually *pee* all over myself?" I cry, bewildered.

Steve gingerly taps the bedding next to me.
"Everything is soaked.
I think your water broke," he says, jumping up.

"Oh my God, you're right. Go get my mother!"

Steve runs from the room.

The pains are much worse now.
It feels like I'm being wrung out like a dishrag.
I let out a whining moan and lie back down on the bed
trying to remember how to breathe through this.
Each contraction punches me in the gut
knocking the wind out of me.
My body has forgotten how to inhale and exhale.
Panic is scrambling up from the bottom of my stomach.

Then my mother is here.

She flips on the light and looks at the bed
"We have to go to the hospital right now."
She rummages through my dresser for a change of clothes.

Then my dad is here too.
"Get her coat, Fred," my mom directs, "and start the car."

Everyone is swirling around me
but I can only focus on the space between my breasts and my knees
which seems to be collapsing in on itself like a black hole.

It takes several starts and stops to get out to the car.
I can't walk during contractions
and then I think I am going to throw up

so Dad grabs a bucket from the kitchen for me to carry.
Then Mom can't find my coat
until Dad points out it is hanging over her arm.

Finally, I lie down in the back seat of the station wagon
still clutching the bucket.
Steve jumps into my car to follow behind us.

It's a thirty-minute drive to the hospital
but Dad is determined to do it in twenty.

Mom notices that my whimpers
are more pronounced and frequent.
She grabs his arm, "Faster, Fred!"

I hope Steve doesn't lose us.

It's called "the labor deck"
because it's a naval hospital.
Everything is named by sailors.
This ship is not well-labeled, and we get lost
soon after leaving the E.R.

My mom pushes me in a wheelchair
through corridors and around corners
feverishly looking
for the labor and delivery.
I feel like we are spinning in circles
and I plead with my mom to hurry up and get there
so I can lie down again.
Somehow she finds it
and I am taken into a small exam room.

A corpsman
dressed in all white scrubs and a small knit beanie
and who looks no older than me
gives me gentle directions.
He tells me to change into a gown
stand on a scale
and give him a urine sample.

Really?!

I moan through it all.
How can I be expected to do these mundane tasks
when I'm being turned inside out?

When I sit on the toilet to collect the requested urine
I notice a bloody stain on my underwear
and turn in panic to look at the waiting corpsman.

This guy, who could be my classmate at GHS, responds calmly
"It's called a bloody show; it's perfectly normal."

Finally he says I can lie on the exam table
to wait for the doctor.
I collapse gratefully and roll into a ball on my side.

Where is Steve?
What if he can't find us?

When the doctor arrives, he becomes the commanding officer.
I've never seen him before tonight.
He does not introduce himself.
He tells me to roll onto my back
which sounds impossible.

"Do I have to? Can't I stay on my side?"
I whine like a toddler.

I don't feel strong
or brave.
I don't think I can do this.

"Well I can't do an exam this way!"
he answers impatiently.

Asshole.

Waiting until the wave of agony subsides a little
I obediently turn to my back and fold my legs
putting my feet flat on the table.

"Can I have something for the pain?" I plead.

"It's too late for that," is his flippant response.

Then turning to the corpsman, he announces
"She's 10 centimeters. Get a gurney.
Now!"

"Find, Steve, Mom," I gasp.
"I want him here.
Please!"

The delivery room
is brightly lit and covered in cool blue tile.
It has the sharp smell of ammonia.

I strain and groan with effort
to slide onto yet another wheeled table.
An efficient nurse works
to strap a fetal monitor around my belly.

Where's Steve?

I search frantically among the identical figures
rushing about the small room.

Please let him be here in time.

She scolds me now.
"You are going to have to cooperate, Miss Dietsch."

Why is she angry with me?
Is there something I should be doing? I've never done this before!

A jolt of fury simmers in my chest
ready to spew from my throat
but all that comes out is a whimper.

Then a sharp sting pulls my focus
to my outstretched arm
as another nurse tapes down the needle
she has just inserted.

I want Steve. Why isn't he here?

I watch as a bead of blood slides over my elbow
and makes a perfectly-shaped scarlet circle
on the clean tile below.

What is that for?
I thought it was too late for drugs.

A third nurse is placing my feet into metal stirrups
and laying a green drape across my legs.
A balloon of terror
begins to inflate in my chest.

Not yet!
I'm not ready!

Then I see him
coming through the swinging doors.

I release my breath in a sob.
Relief relaxes my tense limbs for a moment.
All I can see are his restless eyes
uneasy behind his glasses.
He looks as scared as I am.
He follows the corpsman to a stool
a couple of feet behind my left shoulder
where I can't see him.

The doctor sits on a shorter stool at the bottom of the table
and places his gloved hands on my knees.

The annoyed nurse declares
that she has been unable to get a reading of the fetal heartbeat.

"Well let's get it out then," the doctor says.

Instructions are curt and brief.

"Hold your breath. Push for a count of 10."

I don't know what I'm doing.

"Again."

Just get it out! Pull it out now!
I am screaming
but the only sound that comes out of my mouth
is a shuttering gasp.

"And again."

I can't do this.

I feel Steve's hand
squeezing my shoulder.

One more time, they count.

And I push.

And then the pain is gone
and he's here.

"It's a boy!" announces the doctor.

His skin is dark purple
and his head is covered in matted black hair.
A stubby blue rope
is flopping across his stomach.

A nurse holds out her arms covered in a striped blanket
to receive our baby.
Holding him close to her chest
she rushes him to a clear basin on wheels.

"Is he okay?" I ask.

No one answers me.
I hear only disconnected words
spoken in clipped low voices.

cord

neck

blue

oxygen

I feel Steve's forehead rest against my shoulder.
I reach up and lay my hand
on the back of his bowed head.

Forever
or a moment later
the nurse lays a warm bundle in my arms
and I exclaim in giddy relief.

"He's okay! He's okay!"

Steve is laughing
and coughing back the tears at the same time.
He cups his hand around the baby's head
and leans in to kiss me.

We are a family now.

Our baby
is placed in the incubator
swaddled and capped but still faintly blue
and wheeled quickly through the swinging doors
toward the nursery.

"Stay with him," I say to Steve
my anxiety immediately returning
as soon as our son leaves my sight.

Shortly after Steve is gone
—my father snapping pictures close behind him—
I am returned to the gurney and pushed out into the hall.

I wonder how long they will keep my baby.

And, also
when did my dad find time to grab his camera
and load it with film
in our scramble to get to the car?
Only one hour ago.

Has it really only been *one hour*?

My whole life— *our* whole lives—
have changed.
In a single hour.

A shuddering sigh escapes from my mouth
and I don't know if it's because
I'm terrified
or deliriously happy
or just completely exhausted.
It all feels like a dream.
The kind that I wake up from feeling relieved
but also a little sad, that it's over.

Then my mom is here
holding my hand
telling me, "He is beautiful"

with tears in her eyes.

The teenage corpsman is back
and he rolls me into another small exam room
where I am meant to "recover"
for my new life.

"I've never seen anything like that," he says.
"That's the fastest birth since I've been here!"

I feel proud
even though I know it was not me
in control of my body for the past hour
but the other way around.

Then he tells me that my bladder is very full
and I need to empty it
or I'll have to have a catheter.

I'm surprised since I don't feel
like I have to go at all.

The corpsman holds my hand to help me sit up
and slide off the side of the gurney to the floor.
As soon as my feet touch the tile
a crimson stream splashes to the floor
splattering my legs
and his shoes
and puddling between my feet.

Mortified
I freeze and look at him
helplessly.

"Don't worry about that.
I'll take care of it," he says nonchalantly.
"The bathroom's right there."

My mom takes my arm from him
and helps me walk the few feet to the toilet

a thin bloody trail
drizzling behind me the whole way.

It's still like a dream.
My will feels separated from my body.
Like when you hear the monster coming
and your legs are paralyzed
but you're not really frightened
because you know you're just dreaming.

And in just a few moments
you will wake up.

He finally finds a phone
in a wide hallway under a large, open atrium.
The windows are still black with night.
The corridors are nearly empty
and his steps echo off the white tiled floors.
Jarring fluorescent lights make everything stark.

Desolate.

It is 6:00 a.m. when his Mom answers.

"Kelley had the baby.
It's a boy," Steve says quietly
stuffing his shaking hand into his pocket.

"Okay" is all she says.

He's never felt so alone.

The birth announcement
is made at 7:00 a.m. at Becky's kitchen table.

It's a boy.
His name is Garrott Ian.
He was born at 3:20 a.m.
weighing 7 pounds, 10 ounces
and is only 18 ½ inches long.

Smaller than Steve ever imagined.

Julie and Mark arrive to carpool to school
using every available minute studying
for the Calculus midterm they have today.

"Tell Mr. Knudson I'll have to make up my exam."
Steve says with a tired smile
while passing out the large lollipops from Lamaze class
that Kelley never tasted.

They congratulate him.
And laugh excitedly.
And hug him.
And call him "Daddy".

Steve opens the front door quietly
but Maxi hears him anyway
and runs barking toward him from the kitchen.
She settles down as soon as Steve pats her wiggling back.

He heads toward the stairs to go up to his bedroom
when his mother calls him from the kitchen.

"Steven?"

He stops with his foot on the first step.

"Yeah, it's me," he calls back.
He stands there
waiting
trying to decide if he should go to her
or just head upstairs to bed.

"How's Kelley?" she asks.

Steve turns around and heads to the kitchen.

His mom is seated at the table.
The newspaper is spread out in front of her.

"She's doing good.
She's just really tired," he tells her.
He sits down in the chair across the table from her.
He can smell that she has just come inside
from having a cigarette.

"So it was fast?" she asks
as she gets up and goes to the refrigerator.
She pulls out the jar of orange juice
and pours some into a glass.

"Yeah, after her water broke at 2:00.
He was born a little over an hour later, 3:20."
He accepts the glass of juice
and swallows a couple of mouthfuls.

"I almost didn't make it
to the delivery room in time."

"That is fast," she says.
Then she fixes him a bowl of Honey Nut Cheerios
and sits down across from him again
and watches him eat.

He is careful not to mention any details
about the baby.

And she doesn't ask anything
about his new son.
Her grandson.

Finally she tells him he should try to get a little sleep
and that they can talk more later.
She directs him to go to the basement
where it is dark and quiet
so he won't be disturbed by his brother
getting ready for school.

Taking her advice
he stumbles down the basement steps
and doesn't make it as far as the couch
before he is overcome by exhaustion.
Dropping onto the floor
he is asleep
before he is even aware
of laying his head on the carpet.

I still haven't slept
but brighten immediately
when Steve returns around noon
carrying a bouquet of flowers
and a paper bag of french fries and chicken nuggets
for us to share.
He sets these on the wheeled tray by my bed
and bends over the bassinet, tracing his fingertips
along our baby's smooth cheek
flushed bright pink by his air-filled lungs.
Then he leans in and kisses the top of his fuzzy dark head
inhaling his newborn smell.

He turns to me and smiles.
"He's amazing," he whispers as he dips his head
to lay a gentle kiss on my lips.

When I open my eyes
I can see his are shining with unshed tears.
Nudging me over, he kicks off his sneakers
and climbs up next to me on the bed
which I'm sure is not allowed
but we don't care.

As Steve tells me about going to Becky's
Garrott begins to squirm and mewl.
Steve jumps up from the bed
and carefully lifts the baby from his cot
before he has even begun to cry
as if he's done it a hundred times before.

Cradling his head, Steve gently places Garrott into my arms
and sits down on the bed next to us.
As the snuffling turns to cries
I pull the shoulder of my gown down
and place Garrott at my breast.

Garrott twists and turns his head
while blindly searching for my nipple
with his kitten tongue.

Steve watches intently as I try to help Garrott latch on
the way the nurse has shown me.

"Does it hurt?" he wonders.

"Yeah. I kind of just hold my breath
for the first few seconds."

I squeeze my eyes shut and grimace
as the baby hungrily suckles.

Chuckling, Steve leans in
and kisses Garrott on his velvety head again.
"He's so soft," he breathes.
I smile to see his fatherly tenderness.

Then he looks up at me.
"You're beautiful," he says with awe in his voice.
"I love you."

Then I notice the difference in his face.
He's been so scared and uncertain
for so long.
Now his eyes are bright
with the confidence and peace that you feel
when you know something
is perfectly right.

I lay my head on his shoulder and close my eyes
knowing I still won't sleep.

"Thank you. Thank you for loving me," I sigh.

After school
the visitors start to arrive.
Brian, Julie, Jon, and Susan
bring pink and blue carnations
and a mylar "It's a Boy!" balloon.

I feel a little awkward
in my hospital gown
hastily braided hair
and plain face
but they treat me with something almost like reverence
when I pull back the blankets to give them a peek
of Garrott's dark head and pink cheeks.
They whisper in awe-filled voices
and cover their hands to muffle their delighted laughs
when he stretches his arms or scrunches up his face.

My mom and dad come back too and bring my younger siblings
who take turns holding Garrott and exclaiming at his tiny fingers
and his most definitely Dietsch nose.

Later, more Spoofers come
with little stuffed animals and cards.
Ryan lewdly comments on my breastfeeding
and Steve kicks him out into the hallway.

Steve's parents don't come that day. Or the next one.

They say they don't think they are ready.
I'm not sure what they mean.
Ready for what?

Ready to accept me?
Or Steve being with me?
Or their grandchild?

But I don't ask anything out loud
because I can see
that Steve is trying so hard not to show
how much it hurts.

The first 24 hours I was a mother
I slept very little, but I learned a lot.

1.

After the baby is born
you have to give birth once again a few minutes later
and with far less fanfare
to a large blob
of bloody tissue.

2.

When the doctor sews up the cut that he made in your vagina
(on purpose)
it can actually hurt more
than when you pushed a head the size of a cantaloupe
out of that same hole
only moments before.

3.

The same body
that just inconceivably triumphed over a Herculean trial
is now, just as inexplicably
unfit to fulfill its most routine functions
like walking.
Or peeing.

4.

The process of postpartum recovery
is a perpetual state of red-faced mortification
while your body constantly leaks fluids from various holes
and is witnessed
by family
friends
a string of nameless, nonchalant hospital workers
and your boyfriend.

5.

A mother's breasts
won't have milk to feed her hungrily squalling baby
for several days.
Instead, he will nurse on a thick yellow secretion
that looks like the bile
you spent the first 5 months of your pregnancy vomiting
and leaves mustard-colored stains
on all your clothes.

6.

Breastfeeding is not intuitive
or peaceful.
At least, not at first.
It's complicated
frustrating for mother and child
and hurts like shit.

7.

If you give birth in a teaching hospital
you will be asked to expose your battered vagina
to groups of anonymous men who gather around your bed
and will also request to feel your fundus
"if you don't mind".

8.

Bowel habits of mother and child
including the passing of gas
and tar black stools
are of keen interest to all medical personnel
and must be documented
religiously.

9.

Childbirth can cause
pain
joy
and humility
but there can also be a type of grief
with the loss of a full womb.
The hollow flesh of your abdomen that only hours ago
was firm and alive
with the rolling, pushing, and hiccupping
of the resident within
is now a doughy emptiness
that hangs like a prosthetic appendage.
Gastric bubbles
are the phantom limb of the child
you imagined you knew
but who is actually a stranger
now that he is in your arms.

10.

When your body is torn open by childbirth
it pours out pieces of your heart and soul
along with the bloody fluids
fusing the corporal with the spiritual.
Then it is handed all back into your keeping
in the form of this tiny living vessel
who is in possession of the most fragile part of your being.

It is
a magnificent and terrifying
gift
both from me
and
to me.

APRIL

Three days and a new month later

they say we can go home.
I dress him in tiny red pajamas
with a hatch door that snaps in place over his bottom.
I wrap him in a creamy white knit blanket
with a matching cap that has a pointed tip
and white satin ribbons that I tie under his delicate chin.
He looks like a baby garden gnome.

After he is strapped in his car seat
and we've signed the papers
I'm still a little surprised
that it's not an April Fool's joke
when they let two teenagers
take a brand-new baby
out of the hospital.

Steve drives slowly
in the right lane
with the music turned down low.
I sit in the back next to Garrott's car seat
adjusting the blankets to support his head.
We are both nervous
taking such a precious package
out on the speeding highway.

It seems to take forever to get home.

When we arrive, my family all gathers at the door to greet us
and welcome the newest member of our family.
Everyone wants a turn to hold him.
My mother sits close and shows my brothers
how to support Garrott's bobbling head.

The crib has been set up in a corner of my bedroom.
It is the crib I slept in
and all my brothers and sisters too.
There are scuff marks scraped into the dark wood railings
that my mother says were made by teething toddlers.

Many of the shower gifts I received just a week ago
have been put to use—
pale yellow crib sheets
Winnie the Pooh bumper pads
a musical mobile of colorful plush animals
and the peach afghan my grandmother crocheted for my bed.

Hanging on the wall above the crib
is my large Depeche Mode poster.
Steve nods and smiles in approval.

My mother has added her rocking chair with the cane back and seat
to a corner of my room.
I sit down in it as she carries Garrott to me
fussing to be fed again.

My milk has come in now

and I immediately feel the tingling burn
as Garrott nuzzles at my breast.
Steve sits down on the bed next to me
and rubs Garrott's head as he suckles.

My dad comes in smiling.
"So what do you think?" he asks.
He motions to the crib setup in the corner.

"It's perfect! Thank you!" I answer.

But Dad's smile has faded now
and his jaw is clenched in disapproval.
"He shouldn't be here when you're nursing," he says.

Steve instantly removes his hand from Garrott's head
and places his palms flat on the tops of his thighs.
Looking down at the floor, he is perfectly still and quiet.

He will not oppose my father.

I look from Steve to my dad
and can't decide whether to yell or laugh.
Can my father really still be hoping to maintain
some sense of my modesty?

Then my mom steps in.
Taking my dad's arm, she pulls him toward the door.
"He's the baby's father, Fred. He has every right to be here.
Leave them be."

He doesn't move
until my parents have left us alone.

I can see Steve clench his teeth together
and take several deep breaths.
I can't tell if it's in relief
or in anger.

Then he lifts his hand again
and places it back on the top of our son's head.
He moves his thumb slowly
as he strokes Garrott's wispy dark hair,
careful not to bruise the warm new skin.

"Ignore him," I say. "He's being ridiculous."

He doesn't respond.

Garrott has drifted off to sleep at my breast
so I lift him to my shoulder and start patting and rubbing his back.
He scrooches his face against my neck
and tangles his tiny fingers into the long strands of my hair.

Steve smiles and reaches in with one finger
to pry the hairs from the baby's tight fist.
Gently, Steve wraps his hands around Garrott's tiny chest
and lifts him from my shoulder
placing him on his own.
Steve stands and walks around the room
tracing small circles on our baby's back.
Steve's lips rest gently against Garrott's tiny ear
and I see his lips moving
sharing hushed secrets.

Suddenly Garrott burps
and spits some milk onto Steve's t-shirt.
He chuckles at the baby's furrowed brow
and looks around for something to wipe up the mess.

I jump up with a rag and swap it for the baby

taking Garrott back with me to the rocking chair.
I lay him down on my lap
and clean his face with the hem of my shirt
before lifting him to my other breast.

After only a few days, the motions feel easy and natural.

Steve sits back down on the bed next to me.
He slides his hand under mine
and pulls it toward his chest.

He looks intently into my eyes
and solemnly declares
"I'm going to take care of you. Both of you.
I promise."

The day after we bring Garrott home
is Easter Sunday
and I want to take him to church with my family.

Anticipating I would need it
Mom made me a new Easter dress several weeks ago
that I had agreed to, once I'd finally admitted
there was no point in pretending that I could fit into
any clothes from the Juniors department.
The fabric is a bright green and pink floral calico
and it has a large, white, square bib collar with pink ribbon trim.
It feels like a tent when I put it on now
even though I'm nowhere near back to my normal size.
Mom hands me a wide, white elastic belt from her closet
to cinch the waist, and it works well
still leaving plenty of room for my enlarged breasts
and soft, poofy stomach.

I dress Garrott in a white sleeper
with a small, embroidered yellow chick over his heart.
Tiny silver snaps run from his left foot
all the way up to his chin.
The outfit came with a matching white hat
which I try to fit snugly around his head
by tying the silky ribbons in a tight bow
but it's still a little too big.
His head slips around inside it
so that I have to keep adjusting it when it covers his eyes.

At St. Martin's, I place his carrier beside me on the church pew
and pull the pastel afghan away from his face and arms
so he doesn't get too hot.
I'm excited to have people see my beautiful baby
and I take Garrott out of his seat
to carry with me when I go to communion
even though he never stirs.

After months
of feeling ashamed and embarrassed about my condition
I no longer have any urge to hide.

My baby is so innocent
so precious
so perfect.

And I am so proud
to be his mother.

The baby eats every three hours
around the clock
and spits up half of what he eats immediately afterwards.
He is constantly damp with regurgitated milk.
And pee.
And mustard-colored poop that smells like vinegar.

I try to use the cloth diapers with safety pins and rubber pants
like my mother did, because they're cheaper.
But they always leak.
And I run out of them so quickly, because he's always wet.
And the washing machine shreds them into rags.

In between feedings I try to use a breast pump
that looks like a clown's bicycle horn
and requires me to knead a bulb syringe by hand
for fifteen minutes, trying to reserve a few ounces of milk
for when I have to go to my classes.

Garrott doesn't seem to like the bottle
and is usually wailing with hunger when I return.
When I get home, my mom looks annoyed while he screams
strapped to her chest in a snuggly
as she tries to mop the kitchen floor.

I can't find more than ninety minutes
of sleep at a time overnight.
I'm so exhausted that I can only cry
when Steve comes over after school or work.
He takes Garrott from me and tells me to go to bed
where I fall asleep instantly.

Even Garrott's hungry cries don't wake me
so Steve has to bring him to me
and lay him next to me on the bed.
I nurse him half awake, laying on my side
and then Steve takes him out again to burp and change
letting me sleep until dinner time.

After Garrott is finally put to bed for the night

Steve kisses me goodbye
and heads home to do his homework
and get some sleep himself.

We are mother, father, and child
but we don't feel like a family.

Guys aren't usually very good with babies
and there was no reason to think
things would be different with Steve.
But I guess no one told him that
because he was an amazingly natural dad
from the very first day.

He never looked clumsy or awkward when he held Garrott.
It was as if his son's body was a perfect fit
for his cradled arms.
He quickly developed the perpetual bob and sway
of every parent holding a baby
and never balked from changing smelly diapers
or cleaning the dark, drying stump of his belly button.
He became deft at burping Garrott after feedings
and doesn't seem to be bothered by the spit-up stains
that bloom daily on the shoulders of his t-shirts.

I think Steve's favorite part is napping with Garrott.
Sometimes I notice I haven't seen them for a while
and go looking for them around the house.
I'll find Steve lying on his back on my bed
or on the couch in front of the tv
or stretched out on the living room floor
with Garrott curled up on the middle of his chest.
Tiny arms and legs are tucked tightly under his stomach
and Steve's protective hand cups his son's protruding bottom.
I can hear Steve's long slow breaths
mixing with Garrott's quicker shallow ones.
I pause there and take my own quiet deep breaths
inhaling their peace and contentment.

I think others are surprised
by how easily Steve took on the role of being a father.
But to me, it is an affirmation
of what I've known was in him all along.

Under the reserved and quiet exterior
hide the qualities that make me love him the most.

He is sensitive
gentle
compassionate
and loyal.
And he pours all of these
into loving our baby.

All the fear and confusion
doubt and shame
of the past months just fell away all at once
when Steve met his son.
It all makes sense to him
now that he finally knows what he really wants.

He wants to be Garrott's dad.

They still don't want to meet their grandchild.
They didn't come to see him at the hospital
or my house
and Steve isn't allowed to take him over to their house.

How can they reject their son
and our baby this way?
It is too cruel.

I am angry, and my heart aches for Steve
who is not allowed to express any pride for his beautiful son
in front of his parents.
He spends less and less time at home
only going there to sleep.

Steve told me that his grandmother has declared
that Garrott "will never be a Smith."
I almost laugh.
It's as if she's an aristocratic matriarch, protecting the family name
from the scandal of the wayward heir
begetting a bastard child on the gold-digging housemaid.
Like in a bad romance novel or something.

I don't care.
I already put "Dietsch" on the birth certificate.

They can keep their name.
There are pages of them in the phone book.
I only want one of them.
With or without his name.

Spring Break
for seniors is spent in Daytona.
Or Cancun for those with more money.
And more permissive parents.

I spend spring break
nursing
diapering
holding
bathing
and rocking my baby.

While also attending college classes.

Steve picks up as many shifts as he can at Asbury to pay for
diapers
wipes
ointments
burp cloths
and vaccinations.

The Spoofers come home from the beach a week later
sun-kissed and cheerful, brimming with stories of
sunbathing
dancing
drinking
partying
and hooking up.

They bring a Mickey Mouse outfit with matching ears,
and a tiny, tie-dyed t-shirt spelling "SPIFF" on the back
for the newest and smallest Spoofer.

At two weeks old
we take Garrott to his first appointment with the pediatrician.

I've never gone to a doctor's office for anyone but myself.
I feel self-conscious in the waiting room
nervous that someone might mistake me for the patient.
I technically could be.
It's still three months until my 18th birthday.

I'm not sure how to fill out the forms
since my parents have always done that for me.
I don't even know if my signature on them is legal
so I tell Steve to sign them.
We skip the whole section on health insurance
checking the box that says "None".

How much does a checkup even cost?

A nurse in pink scrubs calls our baby's name
and we follow her into an exam room
painted bright blue with red cabinets.
My stomach flutters like in the moments before a big test.

The nurse asks us to take off all Garrott's clothes
except for his diaper.
He immediately starts squalling when the cool air hits his naked skin.
The nurse talks to him in a high-pitched, cheery voice
reassuring him it will all be over soon
as she expertly manipulates Garrott's flailing limbs
while wielding a tape measure to record all of his measurements.

Then she lays him on a scale that looks like it's for produce
and declares his weight is exactly 8 pounds.
"He's gained some weight!" she declares
and nods at us appreciatively
as if we are fattening a piglet for Sunday dinner.

Steve and I stand awkwardly
against the far end of the examination table
pleased by the strange compliment

and anxious to sooth Garrott's cries
but also too nervous to get in the way of this efficient nurse.

When she declares that the doctor will be with us in a few minutes
I smile as I scoop Garrott up and wrap him in a blanket
relieved the first inspection is complete.

Only a year ago, Steve was one of Dr. Tauntan's patients.
I'm sure that he wasn't expecting to see Steve back in his office
but the doctor doesn't act like he even recognizes Steve.

Dr Tauntan is in his mid-fifties, and his hair is completely white.
He immediately puts us at ease when he shakes each of our hands
smiling brightly like a kind grandfather.

He gently examines Garrott
palpating his stomach and head and checking his reflexes
all the while asking us questions about his habits.

How often is he nursing?
For how long?
How many wet diapers does he have in a day?
What are his bowel movements like?
How is he sleeping?
Does he seem to look you in the face?
Startle at loud noises?

He notes that the dried raisin left from the umbilical cord
has dropped off and healed nicely.
Then he peels back the tape on Garrott's diaper
and declares that it looks like "a nice circ".
Steve and I glance at each other and try to stifle our giggles
feeling bizarrely proud.

Dr. Tauntan declares Garrott completely healthy
and congratulates us on our beautiful baby.

We've received an A+ on our first parenting exam!
This time
I think we have earned our prideful smiles.

Steve is going to Delaware
and I am going to Towson, 60 miles away.

I don't understand why
he would want to go so far away.

> He says
> both of our schools are only an hour from home
> and an hour from each other.
> We can see each other every week.

I don't understand why
he wouldn't want to be together every day.

> He says
> he does.
> He wishes
> we could be.

I don't understand why
he didn't even apply to go to Towson.
He would have gotten in. Easily.

> He says
> It's what his parents want.

I don't understand why
they still don't want him to be with me.

> He says
> that his parents say he is foolish.
> That I could leave him and take our baby
> and he will be left with child support payments
> for 18 years.

> He says
> he is afraid it could be true.

I don't understand why
he doesn't know it is a lie

and that I would never do that.

He says
how can I even know myself
that I won't change my mind about him?

I don't understand why
he thinks I might change
but he won't.

He says
he just knows.
He says
he will always love me.

I don't understand why
his love is more trustworthy
than mine.

MAY

——

On my first Mother's Day
our small group gathers up by the altar of St. Martin's Church
for Garrott's baptism.
It is just my family and Steve, and Brian
who we asked to be Garrott's godfather.

Garrott is dressed in the long white christening gown
my parents bought in Ireland when my siblings and I
"were only a twinkle in my dad's eye".
Now the grandchild they hadn't yet even imagined
compelled my mother to exhume it from its tissue paper-lined box
for the seventh time.

The smiling Deacon Cummins
cheerfully agreed to perform the sacrament
and has arranged for it to be a private ceremony
which is unusual and special.
Maybe he is trying to spare us embarrassment
from the curious stares of other parishioners.

I am wearing one of my mother's dresses, since none of mine fit yet.
It is lipstick pink and long-sleeved, belted at the waist.
It's a style for a grown woman, not a teenager
and is perfect
for who I want to be today.

Steve is wearing his dark suit jacket and burgundy tie
from the Homecoming dance
which are the only dress clothes he has.

His family doesn't go to church
but he comes to mine when I ask him to.

He doesn't know what a sacrament is
or what it means to receive grace.
He doesn't know the words to any prayers
and quietly skips genuflecting or making the sign of the cross.
Still, he doesn't scoff about the "rules"
or question my faith in the bewildering rituals.
Even when I do.

He clasps his hands together and bows his head respectfully.
I think he really does pray, in his own way
in the way most of us do
pleadingly
and with a humble heart.

When the deacon asks us if we reject Satan
and believe in the forgiveness of sins
and life everlasting
Steve responds, "do"
with the rest of us
like they are the magic words
needed to complete the spell.

We share an eager smile when Colleen, the godmother
holds Garrott carefully over the font
from where the deacon scoops a handful of water
and gently dribbles it on our baby's head three times, baptizing him
in the name of the Father,
the Son,
and the Holy Spirit.
We expectantly wait for Garrott's wail
but he is silent
almost pensive looking.

Afterwards, the deacon hands Steve a candle embossed with a dove
and directs him to light it from the large one next to the altar.

"Receive the light of Christ," the deacon says with a tender smile
as Steve cups the flame with his hand.
I wonder if maybe Deacon Cummins means it for Steve
as well as Garrott.

Finally we, the parents, are asked to step forward one at a time
and bow our heads to receive a blessing
under the deacon's outstretched hand.

Our child may not have come to us
at a time or place in our lives of our own choosing
but we don't need the Church to tell us

that this baby who has been placed into our keeping
is a holy blessing.
The performance of ancient prayers and rites
confirms what we already know in our hearts
that he is our very own personal miracle.

We so want to do this right.

He deserves it, no matter
that we are young
and unmarried
and completely unable to support ourselves
much less a child.

I imagine an invisible holy forcefield
descending from above
and resting like a glowing cloak on our heads and shoulders
empowering us with the strength and courage we will need
to keep this promise.

Amen.

We call it the witching hour
but it usually lasts for two or three.
The screaming starts right around dinner time.
Our baby is inconsolable.
Relentless.

His face gets purple
and his eyes are wet with tears
that stream back into his hair.
He stares intensely
focused on nothing I can see.
His arms and legs tremble
and his belly feels hard and rigid.

He won't nurse
and no amount of
walking
bouncing
patting
swaying
shushing
or singing
will calm him.

Steve and I pass him back and forth
changing positions and rooms.

Shhhhhhhhhhhh

shhhhhhhhhhhh

shhhhhhhhhhhh

we croon.

Nothing soothes the changeling child.

It's scary
and I usually cry along with him

                        desperately begging him to show me
                                   what he needs.

One day we discover car ride therapy
and the three of us tool around
the neighborhood streets of Gaithersburg
playing the Homecoming '86 mixtape
over and over again
until our sweet Garrott eventually returns
with flushed cheeks and quick even breaths
pink lips, soft and puckered
like a kiss.

Just like we did last year
we pose for our prom photos
under the blooming dogwood tree.
We stand stiffly and awkwardly
with frozen smiles.

                              Only this year
              six-week-old Garrott is held between us.

              My bubble-skirt dress is lacy and white
                            with sequins on the bodice
                   and seed pearls trimming the collar.
      Steve's tuxedo jacket, cummerbund, and bow tie are all black
                with only his starched white shirt to break it up.
                       We look like it's our wedding day
                 despite the addition of an unexpected infant.

                     My parents will babysit for the evening
                            while we attend the dance.
               I love them for encouraging us to take a night
                            to act like typical teenagers
                   even if we feel unsure if we still belong
                 like when you go back years later and visit
                    your favorite elementary school teacher
                 and she doesn't even remember your name.
            I think they hope that if they give us these moments
                   it will help us chip away at the regrets
                      we have already started accumulating.

Just like last year
we go to dinner with friends.

                                 Only this time
                         we join ten other couples
                    at a Chinese restaurant in Bethesda
                    all seated around a single long table.
                     Steve doesn't like Chinese food
                        and only pretends to eat.

Just like last year
the dance is held in a hot and crowded hotel dining room
with a DJ who won't play our music.
I spend most of the night circling the room
with Julie and Becky, commenting
on the girls' dress choices

Only this year
I am relieved
no one seems to have picked the same one I did.

Like one girl did last year.

Just like last year
we bide our time
until we can leave and have our own party.

Only this year
people seem to look at me too much
and longer than necessary
as if that girl is wearing my dress again
but maybe I'm imagining it.

Just like last year
we take the hotel elevator up to the rented rooms
where there will be beer
and couples taking turns behind locked doors.

Only this time
we won't be spending the night
because I have to get back to Garrott.

My breasts have begun to feel like inflated balloons
filled with hot, wet sand.
They are hard and tender to the touch, throbbing
and ready to burst
like a finger slammed in a door.
I hold my arms away from my body
to keep from brushing against my aching boobs.

Just like last year
I wait impatiently in line for the bathroom.

Only this time
Steve stands guard alongside me
gently rebuffing anyone who threatens
to carelessly careen into me.

And this time
I don't have to pee.

Steve and I lock ourselves inside.
He unzips my dress
and helps me pull my arms out of the tight lacy sleeves.
Peeling the damp fabric down to my waist
I lean over the sink.
Sucking air between my clenched teeth
tears rise to my eyes
as I massage my breast with both hands
coaxing the milk to let down.
Wincing with relief, I feel the fiery pathway opening
and the creamy white liquid slaps the basin
spattering onto my stomach.

Steve watches me in the mirror
and flushes when our eyes meet.
With shame, he turns his back
and leans against the vanity.
I bite my lip to hide my smile.

Just like last year
he wants to touch me, but he doesn't.
Not here at a crowded hotel party
where it's trashy and cliché.

"Hurry up!" a desperate partier shouts through the door.
"I have to piss!"
Just like last year.

Only this time

Steve responds, shouting
"Hey man, find another bathroom.
This one is taken for a while!"

A hysterical snort escapes my throat as I recognize
this ludicrous predicament
as something we have created ourselves
trying to fit our square lives
into the round hole of high school.

Abruptly, I am ready to leave all this
and drop the pretense of normalcy.
I just want to go home
to my baby.

My parents kept my pregnancy a secret too.
They never even told my grandmother.

I think they were afraid of the pain it would cause her.
She has had so much loss and suffering in her life.
They couldn't bear to add any more to it.

My grandfather died suddenly
　　　　leaving her a single mom of four children
　　　　with no income.
And then Gramma began to lose her children.
　　　My dad, the "man of the family"
　　　　　　to the Air Force
　　　　　　　　taking him hundreds of miles from
　　　　　　　　home.
　　　Her oldest daughter, Donna
　　　　　　to the disease of schizophrenia
　　　　　　　　which ravaged her brain
　　　　　　　　so that she was left a shell
　　　　　　　　of her former self.
　　　And her youngest, Shirley
　　　　　　who was mysteriously murdered
　　　　　　　　leaving her six young children
　　　　　　　　motherless.

Gramma got through it all
and is still getting through it
with her faith.
　　　She goes to mass every day
　　　and her home is decorated in crucifixes
　　　and embroidered Bible verses.
　　　A giant wooden rosary is displayed
　　　on the south wall in the basement.

Mom and Dad were afraid
that learning about her teenage grandchild
having a baby out of wedlock
would be devastating to Gramma.
It would be one more thing to grieve.

But it is now clear
that Garrott is a permanent member of our family
so Dad called Gramma up to give her the news
about her first great grandchild.

Once again she surprised me.
"Children are always good news," she said.

Taking life in stride
is another reason Gramma is so resilient, I think.

Then a package arrives for me from Nebraska.
Inside is a quilt stitched together
with dozens of small, brightly-colored squares.

The card says that Gramma made it for Garrott
with all the scraps left from many other sewing projects.
She thought he would like looking at the riot
of patterns and brilliant shades.

I laugh at the collection of clashing boxes
that looks like a big messy mistake.

Kind of like my life.

And her life.

And everyone's.

Also enclosed in the envelope is a ten-dollar bill
and a mass card
indicating that Gramma has asked for prayers to be said
for the blessing of my new family.

Me, Steve, and Garrott.

Somehow
she seems to KNOW
when the rest of us
just HOPE.

It's been two months
and Steve's parents still haven't even seen Garrott.

Sometimes it makes me depressed.
I feel rejected
and I don't understand
why they insist on punishing us
and this beautiful, innocent baby.
How can you not
automatically love Steve's son?
Your own grandchild.

Sometimes I'm angry.
Furious
at their faithlessness
in me
and us.

I scream, "They are selfish and heartless!"

Can't they see
that this is hurting Steve
most of all?

Steve doesn't like to talk about it.
I think he believes
that this is what he deserves.
When I cry and yell, he defends them.

"They are afraid," he says.
"Afraid to love him
and then have him taken away from them."

Their cowardice is no solace to me.

JUNE

———

The GHS class of 1988
graduation ceremony is held at Constitution Hall
in Washington, D.C.
for over 600 graduates.

The Spoofers head downtown early on the Metro
carrying our caps, and wearing our gowns unzipped —
blue for the boys and gold for the girls.
They billow and slap in the wind
a parade of bright sailboats floating down the sidewalk.

It seems appropriate for our class
to have our graduation held in a building
that looks like The White House or The Supreme Court
and is just down the road from both of them.
We've always considered our class special
and destined for great things.

(The fact that
this is where every senior class has graduated
since the student body outgrew the gym years ago
is irrelevant.)

We join the sea of blue and gold robes
and pour up the wide front steps
between the tall white pillars and past the giant wooden doors
where teachers are standing to guide students to their places
and take tickets from friends and family members.

As we enter, the voices and shoes of the excited thousands
echo off the white and black granite floors.
Weaving through the chaotic crowds
we search for our places in line along the wide formal concourse.
Girls on one side of the building, boys on the other
Honor Society students first.

Steve holds my hand
and creates a weaving pathway through the crowded hall
until we find a spot against the wall
alongside Julie, Jenny, Becky, and Susan.

Several teachers pace the hallway, announcing loudly
"Gentlemen, you need to get into line
on the other side of the building.
Immediately!"

Steve kisses me, and before he walks away says
"Look for me at the end.
Bill and I are going to try to be last in line."

I drape the braided honor cords around my neck
and pinch the card with my printed name spelled phonetically

Kelley Marie Dietsch (D-E-E-C-H)

for when it is announced as I cross the stage.

Like everyone, I am jittery with the exhilaration of this moment.
"We made it," we sigh to one another, smiling broadly.

Yes, we did.

        And yet…

                it means something a little different for me
                than for most of my classmates.

They celebrate this day as a rite of passage
from childhood to adulthood.
They look forward to being free
and in charge of their own lives.
I think I mostly skipped that part of adulthood
sometime last summer and dove right into
the responsibilities-and-expectations segment.

But still, I made it too.

I began my senior year with no idea
of how I would come out of it
frantically trying to envision a hopeful future
while grieving the loss of the one I would never have.

I didn't even know
if I was still the person I'd always thought I was.
And I was afraid of who I imagined
others thought I was.

I'm still not sure who I am.

I'm definitely not the same person I was last summer
if the person I considered myself to be then
ever really existed at all.

I'm stronger
braver
less judgmental
more compassionate
more humble
and much wiser
about what it means to love
and be loved.

The me of last year
is still here somewhere
only better
and more true
to the person I hope to become
some day.

I hear the orchestra begin *Pomp and Circumstance*
and our gold line moves forward
meeting up with the boys' blue one.
I link arms with a stranger
and we share a smile of anticipation.

My heart is beating a rhythm faster than the music
as I process down the wide center aisle
following five steps behind Jenny
and searching for my family in the seats above.

I smile broadly, waving frantically when I spot them.
My eyes prickle with tears and my breath shutters

as I inhale the unbridled pride
that rains down on me.

More than excitement
my heart swells with a profound sense
of gratitude.

The graduates
proudly pose for the quickly snapping cameras
feeling like celebrities on the steps of the Hall.
The leather folders bearing our diplomas
are clutched in our hands with our caps.
The guys pump their fists in the air in victory
and the girls wrap their arms around each other's waists
tilting our heads close together.

Gradually, friends break away from our group
to join their families for more photo opportunities
and celebratory lunch reservations.

I have only enough time with Steve
for him to pull me close for one last picture
of just the two of us
before his parents approach, congratulating me
and urging Steve to hurry and come with them
to make their restaurant reservation.

Before he leaves, I pull him into a hug
resting my cheek on his chest
squeezing my arms tightly around his waist.
"We made it," he sighs, swaying us
slowly back and forth like we're dancing.

"I love you," I say.
And then he has to go.

"Smile!" Dad directs, and I oblige automatically
surrounded by my mom and younger siblings
who are anxious to be out of the crowd and get something to eat.

A meal at a restaurant with the whole Dietsch clan
is reserved only for special occasions
so I try to be gracious and enjoy myself, even though
the celebration feels a little hollow
without the ones I love most.

The day feels like summer
sunny blue sky and hot, even before noon.
A perfect day for a walk in the park.
Steve folds Garrott's stroller and drops it in the trunk of the Dart.

To keep him cool, I dress Garrott in only a onesie
printed with blue sailboats flying red flags.
I buckle him in his car seat and kiss his bare toes
and a chubby pink cheek
before closing the door.

Steve pops Erasure's *The Innocents* album
into the tape deck of the car stereo he bought me.
I bounce my head to the lively rhythm as Andy Bell pleads
for *A Little Respect*
while Steve taps the dash like a keyboard.

Before we head to the park
I pull up to the curb in front of Steve's house
so he can run inside and grab his hat and some money.
I wait in the car with Garrott
singing along to *Ship of Fools*
convinced that Andy must have known
about our "baby of the class"
when he wrote those words.

Garrott begins to whine, so I release my seatbelt
and reach around to pop in his pacifier.
What is taking Steve so long?
It's too hot to be sitting out here in the car!

I feel a familiar anger rising in my chest.
Anger at Mr. and Mrs. Smith
for judging me harshly
and turning their backs on their grandchild.

And at Steve
for not being as angry at them as I am.

Andy Bell sings to me about my life.

So precious and so cruel...

So true.

Steve finally comes out of the house and jogs toward the car.
His face is shining.
"Bring him in," he calls beckoning with his hand.
"They said to come inside!"

He goes directly to the door of the back seat
pulls it open and begins to unbuckle Garrott.

"Really?" I ask tentatively. "Are you sure?"
What could have changed their minds so suddenly?

"Yes! They said they want to meet him."

Steve heads back up the front walk
carrying Garrott on his shoulder.

I turn off the car
grab the diaper bag
and hurry to follow them.

By the time I get inside
Steve has already carried Garrott into the kitchen.
I quietly walk up behind him
standing back, in his shadow.

Mr. and Mrs. Smith are huddled closely in front of Steve.
His younger brother, Mark, has come into the room too.

"Oh my God, Steven," his mother says with awe
a tremble in her voice.
Her hands are clasped together in front of her chest
as if in prayer.
"He is so beautiful!" I see the tears shining in her eyes.

Mr. Smith is standing shoulder to shoulder with her
bending in, to peer closely at Garrott cradled in Steve's arms.
"He's pretty big!" he says with a huge grin on his face
clearly impressed by the first sight of his grandson.

"Yeah, he's in the 95th percentile for weight."
Steve proudly provides the stats from Garrott's last checkup
like a coach promoting his star player.

I move a little closer, peeking around Steve's shoulder
hoping to catch a glimpse
of the delighted pride I hear in his voice
as he presents to his family the one thing
that can heal what has been broken.

Garrott just stares at them with his big blue eyes.
His tiny pink tongue pokes out from the tight O of his pursed lips.
Mr. and Mrs. Smith break into laughter, startling Garrott.
Seeing his eyes widen in surprise
Steve quickly places him on his shoulder
patting his back and bouncing him up and down to reassure him
before he has a chance to cry.

I can tell they are shocked
by how comfortable and competent Steve is
caring for his infant son.

I watch
as the wonder on their faces transforms to pride.
Mr. Smith hurries to grab the camera
anxious to capture the moment
when they meet their grandson
and his father
for the first time.

JULY 1988

I am embarrassed to be sitting here
on an industrial hard plastic chair among many others
in the dingy waiting room of the Department of Social Services.
And I'm ashamed of my embarrassment.
I don't like asking for a handout, but I know I have to
if I am going to pay for Garrott's daycare.

That's why everyone in this room is here.
Because they have to be.

I know my parents would give us money
if we asked
and Steve's parents too
but I can't bring myself to admit
that I can't pay for the care of my own child.
They are already giving us so much
and this is something I can do.
Even if I hate it.

Steve and I have a plan now.

We will spend Monday through Friday at school
me at Towson, Steve at Delaware.

We will find Garrott a spot in family day care.
Mom will drop him off in the morning
and Dad will pick him up at the end of the day.
My family will pitch in to take care of him at night—
mostly Mary after school
and then Mom from dinner until bed.

After my last class on Fridays
Mom will make the hour drive to Towson with Garrott
to pick me up for the weekend.
Steve will come home on the train.

I will work at my new job
waiting tables at the Ruby Tuesday restaurant in the mall
Friday night, Saturday night, and Sunday morning.
Steve will work the early shift at Asbury

and take care of Garrott at his house
on the nights I work late.
His parents have set up Steve's old crib in the extra bedroom.

It will be hard.
But we can do it
for four years.

When they finally call my name
I walk haltingly back to the cubical
lugging Garrott in his carrier on my bent arm.

On paper, my situation is clearly precarious.
I'm an unwed mother
and a student
with a part time job.
My poverty is documentable.
The daycare subsidy should be easily approved.

And I should not be surprised
when they offer me more than I ask for.

WIC?
Food stamps?
Medicaid?

> *No.*
> *No.*
> *No.*

I don't need it; I won't take it.
Just childcare subsidy. That's all I really need.
I can do the rest, on my own.

But I'm not doing it on my own. Not really.

Because I have Steve.
And my family.
And the Smiths.
And the Spoofs.

Only because I have all of them, I can do it.

"No, thank you. I don't need anything else.
I have everything I need."

My birthday cake
was made with my favorite Ben and Jerry's ice cream—
New York Super Fudge Chunk—
and a chocolate wreath of Ding Dongs
covered in another layer of chocolate icing.
The hole in the middle is filled with a bottle of champagne.
And instead of candles, two lit sparklers
throw fiery teardrops onto the icing.

I look around the Smiths' kitchen table
as my friends sing "Happy Birthday".
They are all there—
Jenny, Julie, Becky
Brian, Mark, Jon, and Bill.
They are giddy with the surprise they have created for me.
My smile is so wide, my cheeks hurt.

"Make a wish!" Steve demands.
He is holding Garrott in front of his chest.
Garrott's chubby legs pump up and down in excitement
and his blue eyes are wide and round, staring at the glittering lights.

I lean over the cake, close my eyes, and try to think of my wish.
When I open them again, I laugh
knowing it's impossible to blow out these candles.

And that there's really nothing left
to wish for.

Epilogue

But when can you truly say
that the
    happily
        is
            ever after?

I think, for me, the answer is
            never
               and also
                    constantly.

I believe
that loving someone
is like what they say about forgiveness.

It's not an event occurred; it's a decision made
again and again.
You don't just love in a single moment
and then snap a photo, freezing it in place
for years to come.
It is something you have to choose
over and over.

When I chose that our baby would be born, and we decided
that we would be a family
we were choosing the
        happily
            to be
              ever after.

And we selected it again
when Steve transferred to TSU
after only one lonely semester at Delaware.
And yet again, when I told my parents
we couldn't commute home every weekend anymore.
I needed Garrott with me every day.

Then, we decided we wouldn't wait for our bachelor's degrees
to get our marriage certificate.
One week after our sophomore finals

we made public vows
before an altar and under a crucifix
so we could finally stop pretending
to live chastely separate
while passing our son back and forth
between classes.

Of course, choosing to be happy together
is easy
when there are fireworks and confetti.
      The wedding day.
      The phone call
            saying, "We would like to offer you the position."
      The births
           of a little brother
                and then a sister.
      The new car and new house.
      A promotion and a move
           to a bigger house.
      A master's degree
      and a golden statue
           to display on the bookshelf.
      A family trip to
           Disney World
              London
                  Hawaii.
      A 25th anniversary getaway
           to a romantic Greek island.

But it's not only for life's major events.
The decision to love
happens in the small moments too.
When he listens to me
read aloud my favorite parts from a book
and I choose to sit on the couch with him
to cheer on the Washington Capitals.
Each time we are in the car
and he lays his hand in my lap, palm up
and I answer him
by clasping it with my own.

But the sparks and afterglow of these times
can easily be smothered
by the endless collection of forgettable days
that stretch out in between
gradually suffocating the fading embers
like the dust that blankets your shelf of framed photos.

Because most of the living we do
is the repetition of the same
mind-numbing
soul-flattening
minutiae of existing
in the same space
with the same needy humans
day after endless day.

It's
being late for work
because we can't find the other tiny shoe
and the dirty dishes in the sink
that no one else ever seems to notice.
It's
his whiskers on your toothbrush
and that important paper he put on the counter
and you threw away.
It's
the constant negotiation
of the value of a stereo system
versus a new couch
and whether or not a 13-year-old
should be allowed to see a rated R movie.
It's
the impossibility of
touching and holding each other
when all you want to do is sleep
for five more minutes.

More than thirty years later
Steve and I still make that same choice
many times each year, and sometimes
even within a single day
that our life together
truly is the
happily ever after
that we first dreamed it could be
once upon
our senior year.

Acknowledgements

Writing this memoir about my senior year of high school took about as much support as I needed when I was living through it, and from many of the same people.

First, I'd like to thank Jon, who was the project manager of my first draft. His advice to just keep writing every day and then telling me what good progress I was making, whether it was fifty words or a thousand—never asking to read a single one—gave me the motivation I needed to finish in only four months. Well, 25 years and four months.

I want to express my deepest love and gratitude to my amazing parents Fred and Kathy, who read my story, smiled through the tears, and told me they were proud. And also Steve's wonderful parents Susan and Jeff, for not only respecting my need to tell my story the way that I remember it, but for also saying that it is honest, even though it hurts.

Much love to all my siblings who were unceremoniously pushed to the sidelines of my story during that self-centered, crazy year, but nevertheless, quickly scooched over and made more room in their hearts for another brother and a baby nephew.

And a special thank you to my sister Mary who was a very kind and gentle first reader and editor, giving me courage to share my story with others.

I am indebted to my dear friend Julie, who is just as analytical now as she was in high school and still doesn't let a single thing get by her, making her an outstanding editor.

A big "Khouldt!" to all the Spoofers who happily revisited that year with me, searching their memories and old photos to help me fill in the holes. They are still my best friends and my biggest fans, and they helped me to believe that others would find my story to be as interesting as we do.

Thank you to Jim Brewster who has been a very helpful guide and patient publisher.

My heart is full of love and pride for my children: Garrott, Brennen, and Julia, who read their parents' love story and were kind enough not to say "gross" even once.

Thank you to Garrott and Andre for designing the beautiful cover.

And to Steve, who is my reason, inspiration, and happy ending for the story of our senior year; I love you.

Kelley Dietsch Smith lives in Maryland where she is a wife, a mom, and a teacher who loves stories. For many years, she voraciously read other people's stories while a yearning to tell her own kept growing. It finally spilled out into a memoir about a single year of her life, over 30 years ago, that has set the stage for all the years since.